POLITICAL CHOICES
A STUDY OF ELECTIONS AND VOTERS

James Clotfelter
and
Charles L. Prysby
University of North Carolina at Greensboro

D1444782

HOLT, RINEHART AND WINSTON
New York • Chicago • San Francisco • Dallas
Montreal • Toronto • London • Sydney

For Sallie, Ethan, and Justine;
Anita, Nicole, and Michelle

Library of Congress Cataloging in Publication Data

Clotfelder, James.
  Political choices.

  Includes index.   1. Elections—United States.   2. Electioneering—United States.
3. Voting—United States.   I. Prysby, Charles L., joint author.   II. Title.
JK1976.C55   324.973   79-26838
ISBN 0-03-038456-7

Copyright © 1980 by Holt, Rinehart and Winston
All rights reserved
Printed in the United States of America
0 1 2 3 4 5   059   9 8 7 6 5 4 3 2 1

PREFACE

This book combines and integrates the study of American voting behavior with the study of electoral campaigns. It is designed to serve as the text for undergraduate political science courses in voting behavior and elections, or as a supplementary text for undergraduate courses in American government, political parties, and related subjects. The book deals with nonpresidential as well as presidential elections and voting, gives considerable attention to the nomination as well as to the general election stage, and stresses contemporary trends. The style is intended to be nontechnical, and the tabular material can be understood by students without statistical training.

Readers will note that no names of political scientists have been cited in the text of this book. (They are fully cited in the footnotes and the bibliographical notes at the end of each chapter.) No space is devoted to the history of scholarly debates on such questions as the importance of party identification. We believe that for our purposes what is important is the findings themselves and that students are more likely to be confused than edified by discussion of the academic disputes out of which those findings grew.

We would like to thank David M. Olson, William R. Hamilton, Jack W. Hopkins, Murray C. Havens, John Books, and James Seroka for their assistance on various portions of this book, while absolving them of blame in the usual manner. We also want to thank Denise Rathbun for her role in getting this book started.

Greensboro, N.C.

J. C.
C. L. P.

CONTENTS

CHAPTER 1

Why We Are Entering a New Political Age - Maybe

The 1960s and 1970s can be classified as a period of turmoil in American politics, particularly when compared to the placid 1950s. The Watergate Affair, the Vietnamese War, and the civil rights conflicts of these decades highlight a series of extraordinary events in contemporary American political history. Given the importance of elections in American politics, it is not surprising to see the drama of such events reflected in turbulent presidential elections. The 1968 presidential election, occurring at the height of domestic conflict and unrest, nearly went to the House of Representatives for resolution as a result of the candidacy of George Wallace. And the contrast between the lopsided Democratic outcome in the 1964 contest and the landslide Republican victory just eight years later illustrates the volatile nature of politics during this period. But perhaps the most important question, at least from the standpoint of electoral politics, relates not to the particular events of this period but to the future that these events portend. Put simply, do the 1960s and 1970s represent an aberration in the normal nature of American politics, due to unique events of that time, or do they signify fundamental and relatively permanent alterations in the character of American politics?

Although viewpoints naturally vary, most political observers do see the 1960s and 1970s as a period marked by substantial change in the nature of elections and voting. Different interpretations are provided by different analysts, but two interrelated themes are repeatedly stressed: (1) the progressive decline of the party system; and (2) the emerging breakup of the New Deal coalition.

1

The decline of political parties in American politics is suggested by several developments. First, party organizations appear to be playing a less relevant role in election campaigns. Candidates are relying on their own personally assembled staffs and resources, both in obtaining the nomination and in running in the general election. Such changes in campaign methods are matched by an electorate that seems to place less reliance on party labels. Voters increasingly are splitting their tickets—that is, voting for some Democratic candidates and some Republican candidates. Also, when asked which political party they identify with, many more people are claiming to be independent than in the past.

Changes in the party system also are reflected in the breakup of the New Deal coalition. Forged in the 1930s under the leadership of Franklin D. Roosevelt, the New Deal coalition established the basic character of partisan politics for subsequent decades. By adding the allegiance of the urban working class and various Northern ethnic groups to their existing hold on the South, the Democrats transformed themselves into the majority party. Furthermore, the New Deal alignment created party images that remain today: the Democrats generally being seen as the party of the working class, lower income groups, and minorities, and the Republicans being viewed as the party of business, upper income groups, and the privileged. But recent developments suggest, at least to some analysts, that the New Deal alignment is breaking apart. The growth of Republican voting in the South, the weak relationship between social class and voting behavior in recent elections, and the declining political distinctiveness of many ethnic groups are among the factors cited as evidence of such a breakup.

The electoral changes outlined above are often seen as a result, at least in part, of important social and economic changes occurring in American society. Specifically, the development of a postindustrial society is identified as a major source of the political changes we have discussed. The term "postindustrial society" refers to the socioeconomic structure that is emerging in a number of the advanced industrial societies.[1] Perhaps the defining feature of a postindustrial society is the central role of knowledge. The primary emphasis in industrial society is on the production and distribution of manufactured goods, but in postindustrial society the emphasis is on the creation and dissemination of knowledge.[2] The shift to a postindustrial society implies a substantial development of the service sector of the economy, especially such "knowledge industries" as education, computer processing, scientific research, and the mass media.[3] These changes in the socioeconomic structure, along with the high degree of affluence associated with a postindustrial economy, have their political implications. The election issues, political coalitions, and campaign methods that characterize industrial society may be less relevant for a postindustrial society.

If this diagnosis is correct, it suggests that many of the changes in electoral politics that already have occurred will continue. As the characteristics of postindustrial society become more dominant in this country, there will be, some observers argue, further transformations of the political arena. However, there is considerable speculation in this interpretation. Moreover, it often is tempting to exaggerate changes that have occurred and to make inferences that are not fully justified. Before concluding that we are moving into a new political age, we need to consider the supposed changes more carefully and assess the degree to which electoral politics really has undergone fundamental alteration. The remaining sections of this chapter briefly discuss the important aspects of change that will be discussed throughout the book.

CHANGES IN ELECTION CAMPAIGNS

In one clear way, technological development has drastically altered election campaigns. Television is now the most important medium, whereas 30 years ago it was of little consequence. Voters have come to rely increasingly on television for information about election campaigns. Indeed, in 1976 about 90 percent of the adult population indicated that they used television to acquire information about the presidential election.[4] Of course, voters rely on other media as well. Newspapers, for example, were utilized by 73 percent of the people as a source of information about the 1976 campaign.[5] But television is the most popular medium and the one that the majority of people consider the most important.

Television is a source of political information in several ways. The evening news programs of the three networks reach a large national audience, providing at least a summary of important stories. More thorough and sophisticated coverage is available in the various news specials, interview programs, and debates that are broadcast. For the most part, such shows attract a limited audience, but there are some exceptions. The 1976 presidential debates, for example, were watched by tens of millions of Americans. Additionally, there is a great deal of paid political advertising on television. To see the magnitude of this method of reaching the voters, one has only to look at the total expenditures on television advertising by the Democratic and Republican candidates in recent presidential elections: over 13 million dollars in 1968 and over 7 million dollars in 1972.[6] The 1972 expenditure might have been much greater, had it not been for legal restrictions on broadcast expenditures that were enacted in 1971, partly in reaction to the heavy spending in 1968.[7] The heavy use of television advertising extends below the presidential level as well. A general rule is that one-half of campaign expenditures go toward media and advertising, with television costs consuming a sizable share of this.

Many political observers express concern over the great emphasis placed on television in modern election campaigns. Some view the spot political commercial with great alarm, seeing this technique as excessively manipulative. Candidates should not be merchandized, it is argued, in the same fashion that a new brand of soap is. Similar arguments are applied to television news shows. Candidates have too much freedom to create media events and therefore manipulate people's view of the election contest. In sum, television is seen by many as a medium that places too much emphasis on style and image and too little on political substance.

The above criticisms appear frequently, but some research on the political impact of television fails to support these changes. For example, one thorough study of the effects of television in the 1972 presidential election claims that "in almost every instance, the prevailing view of television's role in American presidential elections is wrong."[8] It is quite possible that voters are not easily manipulated by political commercials, and it may be that television supplies considerable campaign information to voters who otherwise would be less well informed.

Whatever the true impact of television on the voters, the increased reliance on television in election campaigns is an established fact. This development is one component of what is seen as a "new style" in election campaigns.[9] Perhaps the central features of modern campaigning are its strong candidate orientation and its independence of traditional party organizations. Rather than relying on the party organization in the state or district, candidates are turning to professionals in the world of marketing and advertising. Professional pollsters, media consultants, advertising men, and other related specialists now are commonly employed in statewide races. And the appeal that these modern campaign organizations make to the voters also is largely independent of the political party. Television advertising, for example, almost always is advertising for a particular candidate, not for a party ticket.

This new style of election campaigning is an expensive one. Total political spending at all levels in 1972 was three times what it was in 1952, an increase far greater than the rise in the consumer price index or the number of votes cast.[10] This tremendous increase in campaign expenditures has led to pressures for reform, and the national and state governments have responded with considerable legislation. Restrictions now exist on the nature and amount of contributions that can be made to a campaign. Also, requirements for public disclosure of the sources of campaign funds are more stringent than used to be the case.

The 1970s have seen considerable legislative action designed to limit and regulate campaign finance. But the enactment of this legislation does not mean that there is a clear consensus on what the problems of campaign financing are and how these problems should be solved. In fact, there is considerable disagreement over these matters. What impact this recent regulation of campaign finance will have on the electoral process is far from clear at this time.

To some extent, these reforms could diminish the importance of party organizations. For example, the public subsidies introduced for presidential campaigns are available to candidates for the Democratic or Republican nomination. An individual seeking the nomination of one of the parties can receive financial support from the national treasury, even if his candidacy has little support from the party organization. In other and more subtle ways, the reforms that have been enacted in the 1970s may contribute to the decline of party organizations. One observer concludes that:

> The decline of established partisan politics is further promoted by developments in campaign finance, most particularly the post-Watergate reform acts of 1974 and 1976. . . . The general effect . . . is to shift money, the most vital resource of politics, from the parties to the control of individual candidates and to nonparty individuals and groups.[11]

THE DECLINE OF POLITICAL PARTIES

The changes in campaign methods that have been discussed suggest that political parties play a less important role in elections today. This development becomes clearer if we look at two important aspects of the electoral process. First, political parties now exercise less control over the nomination process. That is, individuals conceivably can obtain a party's nomination for something as important as a congressional or gubernatorial contest when the regular party organization is opposed to the individual. Second, the electorate now appears to be more independent of political parties. That is, voters less often base their vote on whether the candidate is a Democrat or a Republican.

The basic reason that political party organizations have so little control over the nomination process is the widespread use of primary elections for the nominating process. In most other Western democracies, political parties basically choose their candidates as they see fit. In the United States, political parties do not have that freedom. For example, an individual can enter the gubernatorial primary for a political party, raise his own money and set up his own campaign organization, and become that party's gubernatorial candidate simply by winning the support of a sufficient share of that party's voters who choose to go to the polls. Of course, primary elections have been with us for a long time. Only recently, however, have they become such an effective vehicle for capturing a party's nomination without support from the regular party organization. The development of new campaign methods, particularly the widespread use of television and the reliance on candidate-centered organizations, helps to account for this decreased ability of party organizations to control the nomination process.

Important changes have taken place over the past 30 years in the presidential nominating process. The majority of states now employ some form of primary election in choosing delegates to the national nominating conventions. The use of primaries is a method that tends to weaken the influence of the party organization, at least in comparison to the caucus method of delegate selection. The enactment of legislation that provides for financial subsidies for presidential nominating contests has further weakened the control of party organizations.

The impact of these changes in presidential nominating procedures is illustrated by the 1976 presidential election. Gerald Ford, as the incumbent president, normally would have routinely received the nomination of his party. Moreover, Ford had the support of much of the regular Republican party organization. Neither of these facts prevented Ronald Reagan from seriously challenging Ford. His determination to wrest the nomination from Ford certainly was aided by the fact that the federal government was subsidizing his effort. Reagan's strategy was based on defeating Ford in the primary elections. After some initial defeats, Reagan scored some impressive victories and came within a few convention votes of obtaining the nomination.

On the Democratic side, one also can see the reduced influence of party organizations in the presidential nominating process. A great number of candidates contested for the nomination in 1976. Most of them had only limited support among established party leaders and party regulars. Instead, they counted on favorable showings in primary elections plus financial support from federal subsidies to boost their candidacy. The eventual victor, Jimmy Carter, followed this strategy. Virtually unknown at the start of the primary season, Carter was able to achieve early primary successes, which were then translated into considerable media exposure. Carter's capture of the nomination illustrates how an individual can form his own organization and be a serious contender, despite limited prior national exposure and limited support from the established party organization.

The declining role of political parties in elections also is reflected in the behavior of the voters. The party label that a candidate runs under has less impact on the voters than used to be the case. The phenomenon of voting a straight party ticket was common until recently. Perhaps two-thirds of the voters in 1960 cast a straight Republican or Democratic ballot.[12] By 1972, this practice had declined to the point where only a minority of the voters cast a straight ballot.[13] Furthermore, almost all the ticket splitters in 1972 voted for candidates of both parties in the subpresidential races, so it was not a simple case of many Democrats not supporting McGovern but being loyal to the party for the other offices.[14] Similarly, a sizable majority of those going to the polls in 1976 voted for candidates of both parties.[15]

Ticket splitting at the national level has increased to the point where the carrying power of presidential coattails is very much in doubt. The prevailing view used to be that a strong presidential candidate at the top of the ticket would be a great asset to the congressional candidates of the party. The assumption of a close correspondence between presidential and congressional voting appeared supported by actual election outcomes. In 1952, for example, over 80 percent of the 435 congressional districts went the same way, either straight Democratic or straight Republican, for the presidential and the congressional races.[16] The tendency of districts to split in presidential and congressional voting—that is, go Democratic for one office and Republican for the other —has increased considerably since 1952. In 1972, 44 percent of the districts registered split outcomes, indicating little connection between the two levels.[17] A similar phenomenon exists for senatorial elections as well. There were 33 states with senate elections in 1976, and 15 of them had split presidential–Senate outcomes.[18]

Probing the minds of voters, we find further evidence of the decline of political parties. The proportion of the electorate that is unwilling to clearly identify with a party certainly has increased. Less than one-fourth of the people claimed to be an independent in the 1950s, but this rose to over one-third by the 1970s.[19] Along with this change is a decline in the use of party labels to evaluate candidates, so that voters are less likely now to vote for a candidate simply because he or she is a Democrat or Republican. And not surprisingly, voters do not feel as positively about the parties as they once did. In fact, there has been a substantial increase in the number of people with negative views of both parties.[20]

Despite all the symptoms of the declining role of political parties in American elections, we should be careful not to go too far in assuming that parties are becoming irrelevant. The vast majority of people still indicate at least some tendency to identify with or favor one of the two major parties. Although this psychological attachment may not be strong enough to keep them from voting for candidates of the other party, it does mean that most voters have at least a tendency to support one party at the polls. Candidates are aware of these allegiances and attachments and still attempt to exploit them. For many of the less important and visible offices, the party label may be important. There are undoubtedly a considerable number of people elected to these lower level offices largely on the basis of the party label. Party organizations have not disappeared either. Although candidates may be able to secure the party nomination without help from the party organization, most nominees make a determined attempt to win the support of party leaders and activists for the general election campaign. The role of parties may have declined, but it is premature to conclude that they are no longer important.

A permanently diminished role for political parties certainly would be a significant development. Political parties have been an important part of the system of elections in this country, and our evaluation of the strengths and weaknesses of elections may well be altered by changes in the way party organizations contribute to the electoral process.

CHANGES IN THE ELECTORATE

As the previous section points out, part of the decline of political parties involves the changed behavior of the voters. The growing independence and ticket-splitting that has been observed can be related to other changes within the electorate. A number of developments can be identified, each of which is briefly described below. Taken as a whole, these developments may suggest the emergence of an electorate that is more sophisticated but more volatile.

One trend has been the emergence of issue positions as a central factor in the voting choice. This is particularly true at the presidential level. Earlier studies of voting in presidential elections stressed the lack of concern over issues that characterized most voters. Such things as the personal characteristics of the candidates and the party labels were more important determinants of the vote. Recent studies of presidential voting suggest some change in the motives behind candidate choice. Voters now seem to place more emphasis on issues of government policy in assessing candidates.[21] Because they place less emphasis on the party label, the voters may now be more unpredictable. That is, a traditionally strong Democratic area may support a Republican candidate, and vice versa. The unpredictability of the electorate also could be illustrated by instability of election outcomes from one year to the next. A decisive victory one year by a party in an area may be followed by an equally decisive victory for the other party in the next election.

Closely related to this development is the increasingly ideological nature of the contemporary electorate. Studies of voting behavior in the 1950s found few voters who were at all ideological in their conceptualization of politics.[22] Most people did not use general terms like liberal or conservative to indicate why they liked or disliked a candidate. Moreover, there was little structure to opinions on various issues, as people were likely to be liberal on some points and conservative on others. In other words, knowledge of how an individual felt about one issue provided little indication of how he or she felt about another issue. Over the past two decades, the electorate may have become somewhat more ideological. Such change is illustrated by public opinion data indicating that opinions on political issues have become more interrelated over the past two decades.[23] This increased attitude consistency means that people's opinions are more structured along liberal and conservative lines. There also seems to be an increased tendency for voters to employ abstract political terms, such as liberal or conservative, to explain their candidate preference.[24]

During the 1960s and 1970s the population also increased in political cynicism and distrust. For example, in 1958 about three-fourths of the electorate felt that the government could be trusted to do the right thing at least most of the time; by 1973 only about one-third of the electorate expressed that much confidence in the government.[25] Similar results are found if we look at the confidence people express in various institutions. Negative opinions toward elections, political parties, the Congress, and the Presidency are more widely expressed now than was the case 20 years ago. In general, the American people have become more politically alienated, resulting in voters approaching elections during the 1970s with a considerable lack of confidence in the participants and the process. A more cynical and suspicious electorate probably is a more volatile electorate. At least this will be the case if voters tend to react in a strong and negative fashion to hints of impropriety or dishonesty.

Demographic and social changes also have taken place. Educational levels have risen considerably, and the trend is toward an even more educated electorate. Related to this are the occupational shifts that have occurred: an expansion of the white-collar labor force and a decline in unskilled blue-collar jobs. Further movement toward a postindustrial economy will mean further changes in this direction. These occupational and educational improvements have contributed to the general affluence of the past few decades, an affluence that has led some observers to characterize American society as one where the vast majority of people can be considered middle class. These social and economic changes may mean that traditional economic issues and class divisions are becoming less potent political questions, thereby diminishing the importance of one of the traditional differences between the political parties. Also, the rises in educational levels partially account for the greater issue consciousness and more ideological nature of the con-

temporary electorate. More educated people tend to have more interest in and knowledge about political affairs, and these characteristics
lead to a deeper and more sophisticated view of politics.

Whether the trends described above will continue into the future is
uncertain. Conceivably, the American electorate will become more
ideological and more independent during the 1980s, but it also is possible that the change will be in the opposite direction. Some of the
developments in the electorate may be a result of the particularly
divisive issues of the 1960s and 1970s. A period of relative political calm
might produce an electorate with different characteristics. As the impact of such events as Watergate and the Vietnam war fades with the
passage of time, and as new political issues become more salient, some
of the recent trends could be reversed. At the same time, new issues
and new events may intensify some of the developments of the past two
decades, depending on what the issues and events are.

TOWARD A NEW PARTISAN ALIGNMENT?

The changes that have been discussed above can be interpreted in
different ways. Some political analysts see these changes as symptoms
of an emerging realignment of the party system. By a realignment they
mean a substantial, rapid, and long-lived alteration in the partisan loyalties of the electorate. A realignment would imply significant changes in
the social composition of the base of support for each party and in the
crucial political issues that divide the parties. The political parties
would acquire new and different popular images, as voters changed
their ideas about what the parties stand for and how they differ. Quite
possibly, a realignment would drastically alter the relative strength
of the two parties, perhaps even making Republicans the majority
party.

By many accounts, the conditions seem ripe for a realignment. The
last one occurred in the 1930s. This realignment shaped the present
party system. Prior to the 1930s, the Republicans were the majority
party, but the Depression led to dramatic change in party balances and
alignments. The Republican administration of Herbert Hoover was
blamed for the poor state of the economy, while Democratic proposals
for more active social and economic action by the federal government
drew considerable support. Under the leadership of Franklin Roosevelt,
the Democrats forged the New Deal coalition and established themselves as the majority party. This coalition, characterized by Democratic strength among the working class and ethnic and minority
groups, has remained with us since that time. However, the political
situation has changed greatly since the 1930s, leading some analysts
to believe that the New Deal coalition is not relevant to the contem-

porary situation and that a realignment of the party system is likely to occur.

The increasing independence of the electorate suggests that conditions may be right for realignment. Because relatively few people have strong attachments to a particular party, it would be easier to alter their existing allegiances. Along with this, the growing volatility of the electorate can be interpreted as a sign that the electorate is searching for some new defining cleavage between the parties. The willingness of many voters to support a third party presidential candidate in 1968 and the occurrence of two opposite presidential landslides within eight years can be cited as further evidence of a lack of stability within the electorate.

One can identify certain signs that the New Deal alignment may be breaking apart. A key aspect of the realignment of the 1930s was the introduction of greater class cleavages into the American party system. The tendency for the working class to be disproportionately Democratic has been a regular feature of voting behavior since the 1930s. Recently, there have been indications that these class differences are declining. In the 1972 presidential election there was little difference between middle-class and working-class voters in their presidential selections.[26] Greater class differences did emerge in the 1976 presidential election, however.[27]

Class differences in voting have been modest among the young.[28] Younger voters, lacking direct personal experiences with the Depression and having grown up in an age of affluence, do not respond to politics along class lines like their parents did. This suggests that there may be an even greater weakening of class cleavages in the future.

Other changes also suggest a breakup of the New Deal Democratic coalition. The disproportionate support for the Democratic Party among various ethnic groups has declined substantially. Catholics once were considerably more Democratic than Protestants in their voting. This tendency still exists to some extent, but the differences are smaller. In the 1972 and 1976 presidential elections, for example, Catholics were only about ten percentage points more Democratic than Protestants.[29] Further reduction of this difference may take place. Considerable assimilation of the various European ethnic groups, through intermarriage and geographical movement, has occurred. Assimilation has an economic dimension as well. The upward social movement of many ethnic groups means that they no longer are distinguished by low socioeconomic status.

The South also is losing its political distinctiveness. At one time, the South was solidly Democratic, in both national and state elections. Early inroads into this source of Democratic strength were made by Republican presidential candidates in the 1950s and early 1960s. Following this, Republicans began to register significant gains in nonpresidential races as well. The Democrats remain the dominant party in the South, but Republicans now are competitive in many states and for many offices. Republican senators, congressmen, and governors no longer are unheard of in the South.

These changes in the way social factors relate to voting behavior are due in part to the introduction of new political issues. A set of related issues, which taken together are often referred to as the "social issue," have become more salient in the 1960s and 1970s. This social issue involves questions of social control and morality. Included would be conflicts over what legal restrictions should be placed on abortion, pornographic material, drug usage, and other life-style issues. Also included would be conflicts over how to handle or prevent urban riots, violent protests or demonstrations, and violent crime in general. These issues often cut across existing party divisions. For example, individuals of a relatively high socioeconomic background often are more liberal on such issues than those of lower socioeconomic status. Thus, liberal Democratic candidates might find themselves in agreement with relatively well educated and better-off individuals on some of these social issues, yet on traditional economic issues they would have more support among the less-educated blue-collar workers.[30] The reduction of class differences in voting, and perhaps the growing Republican strength in the South, is due partially to the fact that conservatism on such social issues cuts across party lines.

Another reason for the decline in class polarization may be reduced voter emphasis on the traditional bread-and-butter economic issues that formed the basis of the New Deal realignment. Of course, such issues as dealing with unemployment, regulating private enterprise, providing social welfare benefits, and policing labor–management relations are still with us. But in the 1960s and 1970s these issues did not arouse as much concern and divide people as radically as they once did. Moreover, new economic issues have come to occupy a central role in contemporary politics. Problems of inflation, pollution, and energy sources draw much more attention today. These new issues may divide people in different ways than the old economic issues. The type of people who are liberal on environmental issues may not be the same people who are liberal on labor–management questions, for example.

The introduction of new issues into the political arena has had a particularly divisive impact on the Democratic Party. It was the Democratic Party that was split by the Wallace candidacy in 1968 and divided over the McGovern candidacy in 1972. Increasingly, the Democratic coalition appears too diverse to be held together. In the South, for example, the vastly increased participation of blacks, almost all of whom identify with the Democratic Party, has increased party tensions, due to the presence in the party of considerable numbers of conservative whites. So far, moderate Democrats have been able to hold both the black vote and much of the older white base of support in many Southern states, but in other places Republicans have been able to gather a fair share of what used to be Democratic support.

Divisions within the Democratic Party have been equally present outside the South. The organizational basis of the party is no longer centered so completely on the inner city, on the working class, and on labor unions. New Democratic activists, often middle-class and suburban in character, have been playing a more important role in the party.[31] These newer activists generally are more liberal on social and moral issues, more ideologically oriented, and less willing to compromise on policy positions. Certainly McGovern's base of support drew heavily from this group, and the splits between the McGovern organization and such traditional Democratic groups as labor unions reflected some of the tensions that have plagued the Democratic Party in recent times.

Conflicts within the Democratic Party, changes in the social bases of party support, and the presence of new political issues give many political observers the feeling that fundamental and long-lasting changes are about to occur. One possibility, particularly stressed before Watergate, is the emergence of the Republican Party as the majority party. Drawing on conservative sentiments, particularly on social and racial issues, and aided by considerable defections from the Democratic Party, the Republican Party in this scenario would emerge as the dominant force in the South, Midwest, and West.[32] A related possibility would be the disintegration of both parties and the emergence of a new majority conservative party, drawing support from both of the old parties.[33]

Realignment could just as easily favor the Democratic Party. The basis of party support may be substantially altered, and new coalitions may emerge, but such changes may not benefit the Republicans. The outcome of a future realignment could be a new look for both parties, but no reversal of party strength. Realignment might even solidify Democratic strength and ensure majority status for the party for some time in the future. One possibility is a new "top–bottom" coalition for the Democratic Party: middle-class liberals allied with the poor and the disadvantaged against working- and lower-class conservatives.[34] Such a coalition already has been observed in some elections.[35]

IS REALIGNMENT INEVITABLE?

Perhaps the preceding section has given the impression that a realignment of the political party system is inevitable. Such an impression certainly would be false. It is probably all too easy to assume that the future will be drastically different from the present. But the persistence of the present party system, unaltered by any dramatic changes, also is likely, and attention should be given to the possible dimensions of this alternative. In other words, what will be the nature of American electoral politics if no critical realignment of the party system occurs in the near future?

A look at election patterns throughout the 1970s is required for an adequate understanding of trends in American electoral politics. The data from the late 1960s and early 1970s do not, by themselves, yield an unambiguous picture of future developments. Electoral patterns during the late 1960s and early 1970s clearly depart from earlier tendencies, but whether this departure is a temporary deviation or a permanent alteration is unclear. The character of American politics during the administrations of Lyndon Johnson and Richard Nixon was influenced greatly by the war in Vietnam and the related protest movements, racial turmoil and urban unrest, rapid changes in social and cultural values, and the Watergate scandals. But the primary impact of these events may be limited to that time period. Conceivably, a period of greater political calm will produce political patterns more similar to those of an earlier era. A cautious interpretation of recent election patterns would reserve judgment about a realignment of the party system until additional elections can be observed.

In some ways, the 1976 presidential election indicates a return to earlier election patterns. Carter attempted to appeal to the traditional base of Democratic support, and his attempts generally were successful. Avoiding the party schisms that hurt the Democrats in 1968 and 1972, Carter received the support and endorsement of labor unions, minority group leaders, and southern Democratic politicians. The two previous Democratic presidential nominees were unable to hold such disparate groups together. A look at the social characteristics of the Carter vote also indicates an appeal along the traditional New Deal lines. Carter did better among blue-collar families than among white-collar families, better among lower-income groups than among upper-income groups, better in the South than in the North, and better in large cities than in suburban or rural areas.[36] A comparison of the Carter vote with the McGovern vote in 1972 shows that Carter's support was more similar to the traditional New Deal Democratic pattern.[37]

An inspection of geographical voting patterns in the 1976 elections suggests that earlier predictions of realignment were premature. The belief that Republican strength would increase in the Sunbelt, due to the intensity of conservative sentiments in the region, was not supported by the results of the presidential contest. Carter carried almost all of the states in the South, reversing the trend of growing Republican presidential voting in the area. Below the presidential level, Democrats captured the vast share of elected offices. Following the 1976 elections, Republican control of congressional seats and state government offices in the South was below what it was after the 1972 elections.[38] Republican candidates did capture a greater share of the vote in 1978, but this improved showing at best brought the party's strength in the South back up to what it had been earlier in the decade. This leveling off of Republican electoral strength in the South during the 1970s suggests that future political changes in the South may not be as swift as some analysts predicted.

Congressional patterns throughout the 1970s also indicate that the Democratic New Deal coalition has not disappeared. Democratic congressional candidates have continued to draw support disproportionately from the traditional Democratic groups—the working class in general and union members in particular, Catholics and Jews, and blacks and other nonwhite minority groups. Outside the South, Democratic strength remains urban in character. Democratic congressional candidates dominate within the central cities of the large urban areas, and this domination is especially prevalent in working-class, ethnic, and black neighborhoods.[39]

One reason that the Democratic New Deal coalition has remained together, at least to some extent, is the change in the nature of political issues during the 1970s. The highly divisive issues of the late 1960s and early 1970s have died down, for one reason or another, and various economic issues have become more important. Some of the economic issues in the 1976 presidential election—for example, reducing unemployment, reforming the tax system, or providing national health insurance—are the kind that tend to divide people along class lines. Even in a postindustrial society, politics can pit the economically more privileged against the economically less privileged. And when the important political questions revolve around such basic economic divisions, it is likely that this will be reflected in voting divisions that follow class lines. If economic issues continue to rank high in importance over the next decade, and there is reason to believe that they will, the New Deal coalition may be with us for a while longer.

In the absence of a critical realignment of the political party system, we may expect a continuation of the present situation. This would imply the extension of the New Deal coalition, with the Democratic Party remaining the majority party. But we should expect that the New Deal coalition would persist only in a diluted form. Data from the 1970s indicate precisely this. Even where Democratic candidates have drawn upon the traditional social groups for electoral support, the tendencies have been far weaker than used to be the case. For example, in 1976 Carter did only somewhat better among Catholics, working-class voters, and southerners. In the 1940s and 1950s the splits along class, cultural, and regional lines were much sharper. Similar trends are evident in races for other offices. Even if no further dissolution of the New Deal coalition takes place, the connection between party choice and many social characteristics could be much less pronounced than was once the situation.

Of course, further evaporation of the New Deal coalition might well occur, particularly as a general tendency over a long period of time. This general trend might be marked by periodic weakening and strengthening of the Democratic majority and by periodic reassertion and unraveling of the New Deal coalition. The end result of such a process of change could be a considerably different party system, but the change would not be the sudden and dramatic change that normally is associated with a realignment.

If the future of American electoral politics, at least in its broad outlines, will be basically a continuation of existing trends, then political parties may become even weaker institutions. This possibility implies that party organizations will have only limited control over the nomination of candidates and only a modest role in election campaigns. Instead, candidate-centered organizations will play the major role in the nomination process and the general election. Similarly, parties may exert little influence on the voters, as they will respond largely to candidate appeals. What we may see in the future is not a realignment but further dealignment of the party system. Parties may continue to decline in importance. Election campaigns may become even more candidate oriented. Voters may become even less tied to political parties and even more volatile in their behavior.

Change in American electoral politics over the past two decades has been great enough and unpredictable enough to make any firm statement about the future open to debate. Perhaps there will be further dealignment and further weakening of political parties. Perhaps there will be a critical realignment and a new party system. Perhaps there will be little change from the present situation. All are plausible alternatives. We may not be able to predict the future, but we can gain a better understanding of the likelihood and implications of various possibilities. That is an aim of this book.

THE ELECTORAL PROCESS

Competitive elections are part of most definitions of democracy. The other countries in the world that we normally consider democratic—for example, Great Britain, Sweden, India, Australia, Japan—also have free and open elections. But even in comparison to other democracies, the use of elections to select office holders is extremely widespread in the United States. At the national level, there are 535 seats in the two houses of Congress, plus the presidency and vice presidency. The idea of an elected executive and a bicameral legislature is reflected in the political arrangements of the 50 states, Nebraska excluded.[40] Additionally, most states elect numerous other officials, such as attorney general, secretary of state, and state treasurer. Below the state level are thousands and thousands of local offices that are filled by election. In all, there are some 500,000 elected offices in this country.[41]

Elections are not used only to select office holders. They also are widely used to determine the candidates of the major political parties. Where two or more individuals seek to be the candidate of a given party for a given office, state law commonly provides for a primary election, usually limited in some way to supporters of the party. The winner of the primary election becomes the party's nominee in the general election. Capturing public office thus can require winning two contests, a primary and a general election. By contrast, the various presidential primaries that are held only indirectly affect the choice of a party's nominee, which is determined by a national convention.

Changes in the nature of elections may cause us to modify our evaluation of the role of elections in the American political process. As such things as the behavior of voters, the methods of campaigning, and the rules governing elections undergo change, then our understanding of the meaning and purpose of elections may be altered. Quite possibly, further change in the electoral process will take place during the 1980s, leading to further questions about the role of elections. It is not immediately obvious, however, what significance should be attached to these trends. Are elections becoming increasingly meaningless and irrelevant, or are they taking on new and greater significance? What possible changes might improve the nature of the electoral process? These are questions that our examination of the electoral process will attempt to touch upon.

Questions about the role of elections are important because elections commonly are believed to be a crucial part of the American political process. One sign of this presumed importance is the considerable attention that news media focus on elections. The significance attached to elections derives from the belief that elections provide a means for popular influence on the government. As one analyst states, elections are a "mechanism which permits the largest possible part of the population to influence major decisions by choosing among contenders for political office."[42] Furthermore, elections supposedly make governing officials responsive to the public because these officials have to be periodically re-elected if they wish to continue in office.

However, elections may not fulfill the role assigned to them. The way in which candidates appeal to the voters and the way in which the voters choose between candidates may make popular influence on the government more of an illusion than a fact. Obviously, the mere holding of elections does not guarantee that citizens will have any significant voice in their government. To assess the meaning of elections, we must know how the electoral process actually operates. Such an understanding requires that we dissect the electoral process and examine the specific components.

The remainder of this book attempts to systematically describe, explain, and evaluate the electoral process in the United States. Our description of elections stresses recent developments, discussing in more detail the points touched upon in this chapter. Description leads to explanation, particularly in terms of explaining how the various aspects of elections are related to each other. By identifying these interrelationships, we gain a better understanding of the potential impact that change in one component of the electoral process may have on the process as a whole. Additionally, we evaluate elections from two perspectives. In some places, we examine elections from the viewpoint of candidates and campaign strategists. The relevant questions here is how the behavior of candidates and their organizations is affected by various aspects of the electoral process. We also attempt to evaluate elections in terms of their contribution to the American political process. In this case, the relevant questions deal with how well elections fulfill the functions that we believe they should. Again, our evaluations have an emphasis on current trends, with the aim of aiding our ability to understand future developments in the electoral process.

The following chapters examine the electoral process by following a chronological sequence. Topics are covered more or less in terms of the order in which they occur in an election, although it naturally is impossible to adhere strictly to this approach, as several aspects of the electoral process are interwoven throughout an election. Given our general approach, the logical starting point is with the general context of electoral behavior. Chapters 2 and 3 focus on this general question, examining who votes, how voters decide whom to vote for, and what the significant electoral divisions have been in recent years. Chapter 4 deals with candidate recruitment—who runs for office and why—as well as with some other topics that provide a necessary foundation for further chapters. Chapters 5, 6, and 7 focus on the behavior of candidates and their organizations, taking up both how candidates attempt to obtain the nomination of their political party and how they attempt to win election once they acquire the nomination. The final chapter attempts to tie together many of the points covered throughout the book and to discuss in more detail the potential future directions of the American electoral process.

FOR FURTHER READING

The electoral changes outlined in this chapter are discussed in several lively books aimed at the popular market. The new issues of the 1960s and 1970s are examined by Samuel Lubell, *The Hidden Crisis in American Politics,*[43] and Louis Harris, *The Anguish of Change.*[44] The declining electoral role of political parties is analyzed by David Broder, *The Party's Over,*[45] and Everett Carll Ladd, Jr., *Where Have All the Voters Gone?*[46] Possible new directions in the electoral process are explored by Kevin Phillips, *Mediacracy,*[47] and by several of the articles in *Emerging Coalitions in American Politics,*[48] edited by Seymour Martin Lipset.

NOTES

1. The term was popularized by Daniel Bell. See his *The Coming of Post-Industrial Society* (New York: Basic Books, 1973).

2. Ibid., pp. 18–33.

3. Ibid., pp. 14–18.

4. Bruce D. Bowen, C. Anthony Broh, and Charles L. Prysby, *Voting Behavior: The 1976 Election,* Supplementary Empirical Teaching Units in Political Science (Washington: American Political Science Association, 1978), p. 50.

5. Ibid.

6. For 1972 figures see Herbert E. Alexander, *Financing Politics* (Washington: Congressional Quarterly, 1976), p. 31. For 1968 see Herbert Asher, *Presidential Elections and American Politics: Voters, Candidates, and Campaigns since 1952.* (Homewood, Ill.: Dorsey, 1976), p. 211.

7. Alexander, *Financing Politics,* p. 138.

8. Thomas E. Patterson and Robert D. McClure, *The Unseeing Eye* (New York: Putnam, 1976), p. 21.

9. Robert Agranoff, ed., *The New Style in Election Campaigns* (Boston: Holbrook, 1976), pp. 3–48.

10. Alexander, *Financing Politics,* p. 17.

11. Gerald M. Pomper, "The Decline of Partisan Politics," in Louis Maisel and Joseph Cooper, Eds., *The Impact of the Electoral Process* (Beverly Hills: Sage, 1977), p. 22.

12. Norman H. Nie, Sidney Verba, and John R. Petrocik, *The Changing American Voter* (Cambridge, Mass.: Harvard University, 1976), p. 53.

13. Ibid.

14. Ibid.

15. *The Gallup Opinion Index* (Princeton: Gallup International, 1976), Report No. 137, December 1976, p. 21.

16. Walter Dean Burnham, "American Politics in the 1970s: Beyond Party?" in Louis Maisel and Paul M. Sacks, eds., *The Future of Political Parties* (Beverly Hills: Sage, 1975), p. 249.

17. Ibid.

18. Gerald Pomper, with colleagues, *The Election of 1976: Reports and Interpretations* (New York: McKay, 1977), pp. 89–91.

19. See Table 2.5

20. Nie, Verba, and Petrocik, *The Changing American Voter,* pp. 123–129.

21. Ibid., pp. 164–173.

22. Angus Campbell et al., *The American Voter* (New York: Wiley, 1960), pp. 188–265.

23. Nie, Verba, and Petrocik, *The Changing American Voter,* pp. 123–129.

24. Ibid., pp. 111–116.

25. Asher, *Presidential Elections,* p. 8.

26. Norval D. Glenn, "Class and Party Support in 1972," *The Public Opinion Quarterly,* Vol. XXXIX, No. 1 (Spring 1975), pp. 117–122.

27. Everett Carll Ladd, Jr., with Charles D. Hadley, *Transformations of the American Party System: Political Coalitions from the New Deal to the 1970s.* (2nd ed.: New York: Norton, 1978), pp. 284–288.

28. Paul R. Abramson, *Generational Change in American Politics* (Lexington, Mass.: Lexington Books, 1975)

29. Pomper, *The 1976 Election,* p. 61.

30. Ladd, *Transformations,* pp. 215–221.

31. Richard L. Rubin, *Party Dynamics: The Democratic Coalition and the Politics of Change* (New York: Oxford University, 1976), pp. 98–106.

32. Kevin B. Phillips, *The Emerging Republican Majority* (Garden City, N.Y.: Doubleday, 1971), pp. 461–474.

33. Kevin P. Phillips, *Mediacracy: American Parties and Politics in the Communication Age* (Garden City, N.Y.: Doubleday, 1975), pp. 198–201.

34. Walter Dean Burnham, *Critical Elections and the Mainsprings of American Politics* (New York: Norton, 1970), pp. 158–166.

35. Ibid.

36. Pomper, *The 1976 Election,* pp. 61–62.

37. Ibid.

38. Jack Bass and Walter DeVries, *The Transformation of Southern Politics* (New York: Basic Books, 1976), pp. 34–37.

39. Results of the 1978 elections are summarized in *Congressional Quarterly Almanac,* XXXIV (Washington: Congressional Quarterly, 1978), Appendix B.

40. Nebraska has a unicameral, nonpartisan legislature.

41. Agranoff, *The New Style,* p. 1.

42. Seymour Martin Lipset, *Political Man* (Garden City, N.Y.: Doubleday, 1960), p. 27.

43. New York: Norton, 1970.

44. New York: Norton, 1973.

45. New York: Harper, 1971.

46. New York: Norton, 1977.

47. Garden City, N.Y.: Doubleday, 1975.

48. San Francisco: Institute for Contemporary Studies, 1978.

CHAPTER 2

The Voters

In one sense, election outcomes are easily understood: there are winners and losers. But understanding how and why these outcomes occur is more difficult. To interpret the results of elections, we need to know the sources of individual voting behavior. More generally, we need to understand the psychology and sociology of the vote in order to assess the role of elections in the American political process. Two important questions are relevant to understanding the behavior of the voters. First, what leads some people to go to the polls while others stay home? Second, among those who do vote, what factors affect their decision to support a particular candidate?

WHO VOTES?

Universal suffrage is the norm in American politics, but it has not always been that way. The framers of the Constitution left the question of voter qualifications up to the individual states. In the late eighteenth and early nineteenth centuries, many states had property requirements for voting that substantially restricted the electorate. Furthermore, women were not allowed to vote in most states until the twentieth century. Blacks were denied the right to vote in many states prior to the Civil War, and after the Reconstruction Period, many southern states employed a variety of legal means to limit black voting. Thus, the belief that every adult citizen has the right to vote has not been reflected in legal arrangements over the past two centuries.

Whatever the past practices, the current situation is one of virtually universal suffrage. Property requirements no longer exist, having been dropped during the nineteenth century. The enactment of the Nineteenth Amendment in 1920 ensured women the right to vote. More recently, a combination of legislation and judicial decisions eliminated the legal subterfuges used by southern states to disenfranchise blacks. Furthermore, substantial expansion of the electorate took place in 1971 with the enactment of the Twenty-Sixth Amendment, which extended the federal franchise to 18-year-olds. Very few adult citizens now are legally denied the right to vote. But the small number of people who are not allowed to vote are joined each election by a much larger number of people, often a majority of the adult population, who choose not to vote. The most relevant question about turnout is thus directed toward determining why some people are motivated to vote while others are not. In other words, what motives, characteristics, and situations tend to encourage electoral participation? What motives, characteristics, and situations tend to discourage it?

Turnout in American Elections

The common method for estimating the turnout rate for any given election is to take the number of voters, as reported in the official vote tallies, together with the number of people of voting age, as derived from census figures, and calculate the proportion voting. Applying this method to the 1976 presidential election, we find that there were approximately 81 million voters out of 150 million adults, yielding a turnout rate of about 54 percent.[1] This estimate may be somewhat inaccurate. The official vote tallies may contain some error, perhaps because write-in votes and disqualified ballots were not counted. Also, the census calculations of the number of people of voting age may be inaccurate, and the number of people of voting age but ineligible to vote (for example, aliens or convicted felons) usually is ignored.

Whatever error may be created by using the aggregate election and census statistics to estimate turnout rates, this appears to be the best method available. Surveys or public opinion polls conducted after elections commonly ask respondents whether they voted, but responses to these questions appear to exaggerate the turnout rate. For example, the 1976 election survey conducted by the University of Michigan's Center for Political Studies, one of the foremost election-research organizations in the country, recorded a turnout rate of 71 percent, which is quite different from the 54 percent mentioned earlier.[2] Similarly, the population survey conducted by the Bureau of the Census after the 1972 presidential election found 67 percent of the respondents claiming to have voted in the election, whereas estimates from aggregate election and census statistics placed the turnout at around 56 percent.[3]

The most obvious reason for the higher turnout figures obtained by surveys is overreporting of voting by respondents. Because voting generally is considered socially desirable, respondents may be reluctant to admit their failure to go to the polls. There are additional reasons why surveys may record higher turnout rates. Those excluded from the sampling plan (such as military personnel) or not interviewed for other reasons (for example, those not at home) often are people who tend to have poor records of voting. Also, when respondents are interviewed before and after the election, as they are in some election surveys, the preelection interview stimulates interest in the election and brings to the polls some respondents who otherwise would have not voted.[4] Although the turnout rate reported in surveys cannot be considered accurate, the inflation of the turnout rate probably is spread across the board, so survey data still can be used to identify the characteristics that distinguish voters from nonvoters.

Turnout rates for presidential elections between 1952 and 1976 are presented in Figure 2.1. The highest turnout during this period was the 63 percent recorded in 1960. Since 1960, turnout has gradually declined in presidential elections. The big decline between 1968 and 1972 is due in part to the extension of the vote to 18-year-olds. As we shall see later, young people tend to vote less, so the expansion of the electorate to include those between 18 and 21 years of age depressed turnout

Figure 2.1
TURNOUT IN PRESIDENTIAL ELECTIONS, 1952–1976.

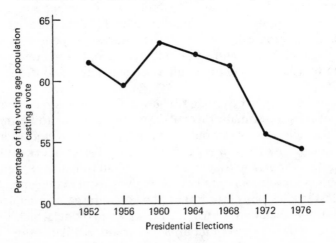

Source: U.S. Bureau of the Census, *The Statistical Abstract of the United States: 1977,* 98th edition. (Washington, D.C.: U.S. Government Printing Office, 1977), p. 508.

below what it otherwise would have been. But even if the minimum voting age had not been lowered, turnout in 1972 still would have been below the 1968 level.[5] This persistent decline carried through 1976, although the drop was less severe than some had feared. Prior to the election, there were predictions that the turnout would be below 50 percent, but the actual rate was only slightly below that of 1972.

Presidential elections attract considerable attention and media coverage. As a consequence of this visibility, they attract more voters than do other elections. Of course, some offices are elected along with the presidency. Every presidential election is accompanied by congressional elections and, in some states and localities, elections for a variety of other offices. Turnout for these concomitant nonpresidential elections generally will not be very different from the presidential turnout rates. Those who go to the polls to vote for president usually vote for the other offices on the ballot as well, although some fall-off in voting does occur as one goes down the ballot.

When congressional, state, or local elections do not coincide with presidential contests, the differences in turnout rates are substantial. Congressional elections held in nonpresidential election years involve less than one-half of the electorate. Only 36 percent voted in the 1974 congressional elections, for example.[6] State elections often have turnout rates just as low, and local elections frequently attract fewer than one-fourth of the eligible adults. Participation in primary elections is equally low. Even presidential primaries, which usually receive considerable media attention, are decided by a minority of the electorate.

Legal Barriers to Voting

Current restrictions on electoral participation are fairly minimal. Legal provisions vary among the states, but commonly excluded are prison inmates, convicted felons, the insane, and other "undesirable" citizens. Residency requirements also keep some from voting, but the impact of these restrictions is no longer very great. Residency requirements now range from 1 to 30 days. Prior to the 1970 Voting Rights Act, residency requirements in many states were longer, sometimes being as much as a full year. In sum, only a small number of adult citizens are legally barred from voting; further reforms in this area, while they might be socially desirable, would not significantly affect the turnout rate.

State laws prohibit only a few from voting, but they discourage many who are eligible from actually voting. Most important are the laws and procedures governing registration, which is required of those desiring to vote in most areas of the country.[7] The justification for voter registration is the prevention of electoral fraud. Requiring registration prior to the election allows officials to check the qualifications of those registered and prevent the ineligible from voting. Whatever the impact on preventing electoral fraud, registration procedures do have a great impact, intended or unintended, on the likelihood of citizens actually registering:

> Registration locations could be too few and undermanned. Hours could be inconvenient, beginning after most people had gone to work and closing before they had come home. The enrolling places could be underpublicized and registration periods could be kept to a minimum by law or held so far in advance of elections that few would have the motivation to vote. . . . In rural areas, registration offices could be located far from population centers, too far for a reasonable person to travel to perform a ritualistic duty. Prospective registrants could be kept in long waiting lines and subjected to embarrassing questions in public about their qualifications. The enrolling places themselves could be difficult to find—the back room of the third floor of a school building—to discourage all but the most perservering.[8]

Studies of turnout rates indicate the considerable relevance of registration procedures. One examination of differences in turnout rates among cities concluded that the variation in turnout rates was very strongly related to the variation in registration rates:

> . . . the relationship was almost one-to-one; that is, if the percentage of the population of voting age registered to vote in city A was one percent higher than in city B, then the percentage of the population of voting age actually voting in city A was, on the average, almost exactly one percent higher than in city B.[9]

The differences in local registration rates, in turn, reflect "local differences in the rules governing, and arrangements for handling, the registration of voters."[10]

A similar conclusion was reached in a study of turnout in the 1972 presidential election. An analysis of the impact of state registration laws found a clear relationship between turnout and several aspects of registration procedures. Specifically, turnout was increased by: (a) having the closing date for registration nearer to election day; (b) having the registration offices open more hours during the week, particularly evening and Saturday hours; and (c) allowing for absentee registration.[11] The estimated impact of these laws was substantial; if all states had established registration procedures as permissive as the least restrictive states, turnout would have been about nine percentage points greater.[12]

In general, registration procedures affect turnout by requiring potential voters to acquire information and spend time registering. The more information that people have to acquire to learn how and where to register and the more time and inconvenience that is involved in registering, the less likely it is that people will register. These tendencies apply particularly to those with marginal levels of motivation. Those highly motivated to vote will register even if it is inconvenient and difficult to do so. Those with no interest in voting will not bother to register regardless of how easy it is. But those falling between these two extremes may or may not register, depending on the difficulty involved.

Several proposals to reform registration procedures have been made. President Carter, for example, proposed a system of postcard registration. This and other similar schemes are based on a simple idea: the turnout rate can be boosted by lessening the difficulty of registering. If such proposals were adopted, they would bring the United States close to the procedures prevalent in European democracies. In most of those countries, the government actively attempts to register all eligible adult citizens. Consequently, European turnout rates are significantly higher than those found in the U.S.

Motives for Voting

The most important reason why people vote is that they are interested in and concerned about the election.[13] For any given election, there will be considerable variation in these feelings among the electorate. Some will be extremely interested in the election campaign and very concerned about the election outcome, while others will feel quite the opposite. The relationship of electoral participation to interest in the election is illustrated by the data in Table 2.1. Drawing on information from a survey of the electorate at the time of the 1976 presidential election, we can examine the reported voting behavior of respondents according to their level of interest in the election campaign. The data

TABLE 2.1. Turnout in the 1976 Presidential Election by Political Interest

	Political Interest		
	Low	Medium	High
Percent voting in the 1976 election	47	72	84
(N)	(475)	(1014)	(902)

The percentages represent the respondents in each category of political interest who claimed to have voted in the 1976 election. The numbers in parentheses indicated the total number of respondents in each category.

Source: Calculated from data provided by Bruce D. Bowen, C. Anthony Broh, and Charles L. Prysby, Voting Behavior: The 1976 Election, Supplementary Empirical Teaching Units in Political Science (Washington: American Political Science Association, 1978).

in Table 2.1 show that those who were more interested in the election were more likely to vote. Similar results would be obtained if we looked at the connection between voting and concern over the outcome of the election, which tends to be strongly related to interest in the election campaign.

Considerable interest in an election tends to be a reflection of a more general psychological involvement in politics. People vary considerably on this dimension, with some being extremely absorbed in the political events that surround them and others having no interest in or aware-ness of the political world. More of those whose general psychological involvement in politics is high tend to follow account of politics in the news media, to seek out political information, to talk about political matters, and to participate in politics in a variety of ways. Although an individual with low political involvement in general might become highly interested in a particular election, the tendency is for interest in a specific election to be related to general psychological involvement in politics.

The relationship of electoral participation to interest in and concern about the election helps to explain why turnout differs among the vari-ous types of elections. Presidential elections have the highest turnout rates because more people are interested in the campaign and con-cerned about the outcome. Voters display less interest in and concern about the less visible offices. Hence, turnout rates for elections for the less important offices will be lower. The interest in the election for a given office also may change over time, causing the turnout rate to fluctuate. The election for a specifc congressional seat, for example, might evoke more interest and concern, and therefore higher turnout, in one year than in the next, depending on the candidates and issues involved.

Related to psychological involvement in politics is the concept of political efficacy. Political efficacy refers to the belief that "the affairs of government can be understood and influenced by individual citi-zens."[14] Individuals with a strong sense of political efficacy feel that they and others like them can affect what the government does. Those with a weak sense of political efficacy feel that they lack the ability to influence governing officials or that governing officials are unresponsive to the people. Individuals with higher levels of political efficacy are more likely to vote. Data from the 1972 presidential election can be used to illustrate this relationship; the relevant information is presented in Table 2.2, and one can see the difference between the more and less efficacious. Political efficacy and psychological involvement in politics are related; the more involved tend to be more efficacious. But the relationship is far from perfect, and each variable exercises a separate and independent effect on the likelihood of voting.

The decline in turnout mentioned earlier in this chapter may be a reflection of declining levels of political efficacy. The results of a variety of public opinion polls and surveys indicate that since the mid-1960s trust in government has declined and political cynicism has increased.[15] If people have become more distrustful of and cynical about their political institutions, it is likely that they feel less politically efficacious. Thus, the decline in electoral participation that has occurred during the 1960s and 1970s may be a result of more negative attitudes toward the political process.

TABLE 2.2. Turnout in the 1972 Presidential Election by Political Efficacy

	Political Efficacy		
	Low	Medium	High
Percent voting in the 1972 election	63	78	84
(N)	(1071)	(413)	(788)

The figures represent the percentages of respondents in each category of political efficacy who claimed to have voted in the 1972 election. The numbers in parentheses indicate the total number of respondents in each category.

Source: Calculated from data provided by Bruce D. Bowen, C. Anthony Broh, and Charles L. Prysby, Voting Behavior: The 1972 Election, Supplementary Empirical Teaching Units in Political Science (Washington: American Political Science Associaton, 1975).

A third motive for voting is the belief that one should go to the polls as a matter of civic duty.[16] Feelings differ on this dimension. Many people feel a strong responsibility to vote, but others do not feel any strong obligation to do so. Those who feel strongly that a citizen has a responsibility to vote are highly likely to cast a ballot. Nonvoters, on the other hand, are likely to come from the ranks of those who feel no special obligation to vote. This relationship can be illustrated by survey data collected during the 1976 election. Respondents were asked several questions about the importance of voting; from their responses to these questions we can determine their sense of obligation to vote. The data in Table 2.3 show that those with a stronger sense of civic duty are more likely to actually go to the polls.

In sum, voting is related to being interested in and concerned about the election, to having a strong sense of political efficacy, and to feeling that voting is a civic responsibility. Still, this provides only a partial explanation of why some vote while others do not. Some people have the above feelings, yet fail to go to the polls. Others show up even though they lack such feelings. Perhaps voting is in part idiosyncratic.[17] Taken as a whole, however, there are some predictable differences in attitudes between voters and nonvoters.

TABLE 2.3. Turnout in the 1976 Presidential Election by Sense of Civic Duty

	Sense of Civic Duty	
	Weak	Strong
Percent voting in the 1976 election	64	84
(N)	(1022)	(1105)

The figures represent the percentages of respondents in each category of sense of civic duty who claimed to have voted in the 1976 election. The numbers in parentheses indicate the total number of respondents in each category. Sense of civic duty was measured by responses to four questions about the importance of voting.

Source: Calculated from data presented in Bruce A. Campbell, The American Electorate (New York: Holt, Rinehart and Winston, 1979), p. 238.

Social Characteristics of Voters

The psychological sources of electoral participation are not evenly or randomly distributed across the population. For a number of reasons, these psychological factors are related to several social or demographic characteristics. Thus, turnout rates differ among social groups, and those who vote are socially or demographically unrepresentative of the entire adult population.

The most important social characteristic affecting the likelihood of voting is the individual's socioeconomic status. This relationship has been repeatedly established by research studies, and it holds true whether education, occupation, or income is used as the indicator of social status. Of the various aspects of socioeconomic status, education is the most important influence on electoral participation. The relationship of education to voting in the 1976 presidential election is evident in the data presented in Table 2.4; about 60 percent of those with a grade-school education reported voting in the election, compared to 85 percent of those with a college education.

There are several reasons why education is so strongly related to turnout. Formal education imparts information about politics and related fields. It also develops learning skills that make it easier to comprehend political questions. For these reasons, more educated people tend to have higher levels of political interest and efficacy, and therefore higher turnout rates. It may also be that the type of people who choose to become highly educated are the type of people who would be more likely to vote anyway, perhaps because of their family background or their personality characteristics. Finally, schools are a place where individuals are socialized into accepting basic values, among which probably would be a sense of civic responsibility or obligation.

TABLE 2.4. Turnout in the 1976 Presidential Election by Education

	Education		
	Grade School	High School	College
Percent voting in the 1976 election	60	66	85
(N)	(376)	(1189)	(830)

The percentages represent the respondents in each category of education who claimed to have voted in the 1976 election. The numbers in parentheses indicate the total number of respondents in each category.

Source: Calculated from data provided by Bruce D. Bowen, C. Anthony Broh, and Charles L. Prysby, Voting Behavior: The 1976 Election, Supplementary Empirical Teaching Units in Political Science (Washington: American Political Science Association, 1978).

More highly educated people tend to have higher incomes and more prestigious occupations, so part of the relationship between turnout and these other aspects of social status is due to the impact of education. But occupation and income exercise some influence of their own. White-collar occupations, more than blue-collar occupations, provide information or skills that make politics more understandable. Individuals in certain occupations, such as farmers or government employees, are particulatly affected by governmental policies. Insofar as occupation heightens political interest and efficacy, it affects the likelihood of voting. Income probably has less impact on voting, apart from its obvious connection to education and occupation, but some means of influence can be suggested. Other things being equal, a higher income probably leads to a greater feeling of a stake in the system, a greater sense of political efficacy, and a greater sense of civic obligation.

Several social and demographic characteristics are related to electoral participation simply because they are linked to socioeconomic status. Race is one example. Even after the elimination of legal barriers to black voting, the black turnout rate has remained below that of whites. The difference, however, is solely attributable to racial differences in education, occupation, and income. When blacks and whites of similar socioeconomic status are compared, we find that blacks are equally likely to vote.[18]

Besides socioeconomic status, the other important factor that affects the likelihood of voting is age. Young adults are less likely to go to the polls, and turnout increases with age until relatively late in life, when there is a small dropoff. Figure 2.2 shows the relationship between age and voting in the 1976 presidential election, and the observed pattern illustrates the general tendencies that have been found by a number of studies. The lower turnout among younger citizens probably reflects

Figure 2.2
TURNOUT IN THE 1976 PRESIDENTIAL ELECTION BY AGE.

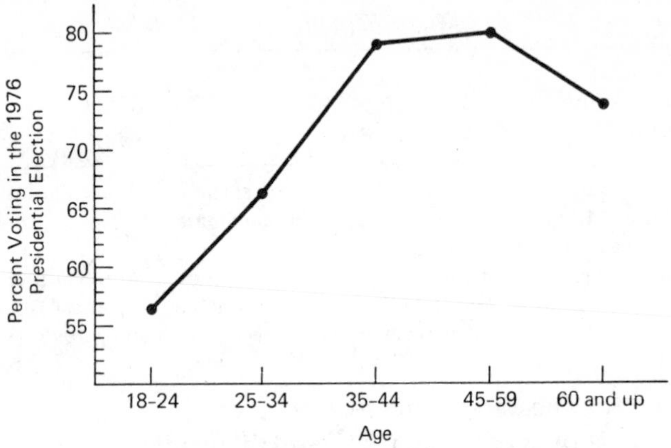

Source: Calculated from data provided by Bruce D. Bowen, C. Anthony Broh, and Charles L. Prysby, *Voting Behavior: The 1976 Election,* Supplementary Empirical Teaching Units in Political Science (Washington, D.C.: American Political Science Association, 1978).

the fact that (a) they are more geographically mobile and less integrated into a community and (b) they are still in the process of acquiring information about and developing interest in politics. The decline in participation among the elderly reflects the infirmities associated with old age.[19]

Other social and demographic characteristics do not exercise very much direct influence on electoral participation. Turnout rates for men are slightly higher than for women, reflecting in part cultural values about sex roles, but also reflecting socioeconomic and age differences (for example, there are more older, poorly educated women). Catholics tend to vote more than Protestants, and urban residents turn out more than those in rural areas, but these differences are primarily a result of other differences. In general, once age, education, and occupation are taken into account, the remaining social and demographic characteristics are not strongly related to whether or not one votes.

Significance of Turnout Rates

Some observers see the failure of many people to vote as an indication of serious political problems. Low turnout rates are interpreted as a symptom of apathy and alienation, two characteristics that do not correspond to the ideals of democratic theory. Especially significant is the decline in turnout during the 1960s and 1970s, as this suggests that the electorate is becoming more apathetic and alienated. Moreover, the turnout rates in the United States often are compared unfavorably to the higher rates in many other Western democracies. Whatever the proper interpretation of nonvoting, considerable concern over this phenomenon exists, and efforts to increase electoral participation are likely to be made.

Low turnout rates are significant in another way. Those who vote are, in social and demographic terms, different from those who do not. If the electorate is socially unrepresentative of the population, it may be politically unrepresentative as well. This is particularly likely when the turnout rate is low, as it often is for primary, local, and state elections. If turnout rates were higher, the types of candidates elected, and thus the types of government policies enacted, might be different.

From the standpoint of the candidate, failure of many people to vote has another significance. It means that the candidate and his organization need to worry about getting their likely supporters registered and to the polls. Considerable campaign effort frequently is directed to this task, although it is often difficult to determine how to maximize the turnout of one's supporters while minimizing the turnout of the supporters of other candidates. The outcome of an election, it should be remembered, depends not on what the people think but on what the voters say.

PARTY IDENTIFICATION

Studies of electoral behavior have emphasized the role of party identification, a concept that refers to a psychological attachment to a political party. For the individual, an attachment to a party may make it easier to understand and evaluate political information by providing a reference point. In this sense, party identification is a perceptual screen through which the voter perceives politics. For example, a Democratic voter may respond one way toward a policy advocated by a Republican candidate, but a different way if the same policy is advocated by a Democratic candidate.

At the aggregate level, party identification provides a basis for judging the impact of short-term and long-term forces in an election. The shifts in party identification over time for a population indicate the trends and developments in basic party loyalties. An analysis of the results of specific elections, relative to what would be expected on the basis of partisan loyalties, provides a measure of the impact of the events and circumstances associated with each election. This distinction between general trends (long-term forces) and factors specific to a given election (short-term forces) is a useful one.

Partisan Attachments

Surveys of the electorate have measured party identification with uncomplicated and direct questions, such as the ones used by the University of Michigan's Center for Political Studies:

"Generally speaking, do you usually think of yourself as a Republican, a Democrat, an independent, or what?" Those identifying as a Republican or a Democrat are asked "Would you call yourself a strong Republican (Democrat) or a not very strong Republican (Democrat)?" Those responding to the first question by claiming they were independents are asked "Do you think of yourself as closer to the Republican or to the Democratic Party?"[20]

Responses to the full set of questions permit a sevenfold classification:
1. Strong Democrats;
2. Weak Democrats;
3. Independents leaning toward the Democrats;
4. Independents not closer to either party;
5. Independents leaning toward the Republicans;
6. Weak Republicans;
7. Strong Republicans.

For certain purposes, it will be appropriate to use this complete classification. In other cases it will be useful to simplify matters by reducing the number of categories. To do this, we will employ a three-fold classification of Democrats, Republicans, and independents. The Democratic and Republican categories will include all those who express some attachment to the respective political party, including the independent leaners; the independent category will include only the pure independents. This will allow us to make a simple comparison between people with some psychological attachment to the Democratic Party and people with some psychological attachment to the Republican Party.

The distribution of party identification in presidential election years from 1952 to 1976 is presented in Table 2.5. As one can see, throughout this period, the Democrats have been the majority party in the sense of having more identifiers. The size of this Democratic advantage has varied, but it has always been substantial. If we include the independent leaners, the proportion of people expressing an attachment to the Democrats has ranged from 51 percent to 60 percent. Republican identifiers plus leaners have totaled no more than 37 percent of the population and as little as 30 percent.

The stability of the partisan attachments in the aggregate is apparent in Table 2.5. The shifts over any four-year period are relatively small. For example, between 1972 and 1976 there was at most a 1 percentage

TABLE 2.5. Party Identification in Presidential Election Years, 1952–1976

	Years						
	1952	1956	1960	1964	1968	1972	1976
Strong Democrat	22	21	21	26	20	15	15
Weak Democrat	25	23	25	25	25	25	25
Independent Democrat	10	7	8	9	10	11	12
Independent	5	9	8	8	11	13	14
Independent Republican	7	8	7	6	9	11	10
Weak Republican	14	14	13	13	14	13	14
Strong Republican	13	15	14	11	10	10	9
Apolitical; Don't Know	4	3	4	2	1	2	1
Total	100	100	100	100	100	100	100

The numbers in each column indicate the estimated percentage distribution of party identification for the U.S. adult population in that year.

Source: Election year surveys conducted by the Survey Research Center/Center for Political Studies at the University of Michigan.

point change in each of the seven categories of party identification. The largest change over a four-year period in any category is the 6 percentage point decline in strong Democrats between 1964 and 1968. But while the short-term shifts are relatively small, there has been a significant trend during the 1960s and 1970s. People are increasingly thinking of themselves as independents. In 1964 less than one-fourth of the population claimed to be an independent (all types), but over one-third did so in 1976. And those who identify with a party now are more likely to consider themselves weak partisans. Strong partisans have dropped from over one-third of the population in 1964 to less than one-fourth in 1976. This declining partisanship is an important development, and it will be discussed in more depth in subsequent sections.

Party Identification and Voting Behavior

Party identification is not synonymous with voting behavior. A comparison of the distribution of party identification with the results of presidential elections from 1952 to 1976 (see Table 2.6) illustrates this point. Throughout this period, the Democrats have been the majority party, yet the Republicans have won four of the seven presidential contests. Both Eisenhower and Nixon were elected and reelected with the help of votes from Democratic identifiers.

The presidential voting patterns of Democratic, Republican, and independent identifiers from 1960 to 1976 are presented in Table 2.7. Looking at this table, we see that in every year there are some voters who identify with one party yet cast a ballot for the candidate of the

TABLE 2.6.   Results of Presidential Elections, 1952–1976

	Percentage of Popular Vote	Electoral Vote
1952		
Dwight D. Eisenhower (R)	55.1	442
Adlai E. Stevenson (D)	44.4	89
Other	.5	—
1956		
Dwight D. Eisenhower (R)	57.4	457
Adlai E. Stevenson (D)	42.0	74
Other	.6	—
1960		
John F. Kennedy (D)	49.7	303
Richard M. Nixon (R)	49.5	219
Other	.8	15
1964		
Lyndon B. Johnson (D)	61.1	486
Barry M. Goldwater (R)	38.5	52
Other	.5	—
1968		
Richard M. Nixon	43.4	301
Hubert H. Humphrey (D)	42.7	191
George C. Wallace (AI)	13.5	46
Other	.4	—
1972		
Richard M. Nixon (R)	60.7	520
George S. McGovern (D)	37.5	17
Other	1.8	1
1976		
Jimmy E. Carter (D)	50.1	297
Gerald R. Ford (R)	48.0	240
Other	1.9	1

Source: U.S. Bureau of the Census, *The Statistical Abstract of the United States: 1977,* 98th edition (Washington, D.C.: U.S. Government Printing Office, 1977), pp. 492, 495; and *Elections '76* (Washington, D.C.: Congressional Quarterly, 1976), pp. 104–105.

other party. Defection rates were particularly high among Republicans in 1964 and among Democrats in 1972, both landslide elections. In the more evenly divided 1960 and 1976 elections, voting was more along party lines.

If we make finer distinctions among voters, we find that the strong partisans are more likely than the weak partisans and independent leaners to vote for the candidate of their party. Party identification may thus be viewed as a continuum on which the likelihood of voting Democratic decreases (and the likelihood of voting Republican increases) as one moves from the strong Democratic end of the continuum toward the strong Republican end. The one qualification to this conceptualization is that the weak partisans and independent leaners do not differ much from each other in the way that they vote. In other words, the electoral behavior of weak Democrats and independent Democrats is similar, and the same holds for weak Republicans and independent Republicans. This is clear if we look at the data in Tables 2.8 and 2.9, which contain the presidential and congressional voting patterns in 1972 and 1976 for each category of party identification.

An inspection of the data in Table 2.7 reveals that the independent vote, as compared to the votes of partisans, fluctuates more from one election to the next. This greater volatility of independents, combined

TABLE 2.7. Presidential Vote by Party Identification, 1960–1976

Presidential Vote	Party Identification		
	Democratic	Independent	Republican
1960			
Kennedy (D)	82	46	8
Nixon (R)	18	54	92
	100	100	100
1964			
Johnson (D)	89	77	27
Goldwater (R)	11	23	73
	100	100	100
1968			
Nixon (R)	20	56	87
Humphrey (D)	68	24	6
Wallace (AI)	12	20	7
	100	100	100
1972			
Nixon (R)	42	70	92
McGovern (D)	58	30	8
	100	100	100
1976			
Carter (D)	81	43	14
Ford (R)	19	57	86
	100	100	100

The Democratic category includes all those identifying with or leaning toward the Democratic Party. The Republican category includes all those identifying with or leaning toward the Republican Party. Those not voting or voting for minor candidates are excluded from this table.

Source: Election year surveys conducted by Survey Research Center/Center for Political Studies, University of Michigan.

TABLE 2.8 Presidential and Congressional Vote by Party Identificaton, 1972

| | Party Identification | | | | | | |
| | Democratic | | | Independent | Republican | | |
	Strong	Weak	Independent	Independent	Independent	Weak	Strong
Presidential election: percent voting for							
Nixon (R)	27	52	39	70	87	91	97
McGovern (D)	73	48	61	30	13	9	3
	100	100	100	100	100	100	100
(N)	(252)	(396)	(160)	(130)	(184)	(247)	(211)
Congressional election: percent voting for							
Democratic Candidate	92	81	79	56	27	24	15
Republican Candidate	8	19	21	44	73	76	85
	100	100	100	100	100	100	100
(N)	(210)	(324)	(132)	(112)	(150)	(217)	(186)

Figures represent the percent voting for the specified candidate for each category of party identification. The number of respondents in the category is in parentheses. Nonvoters and those voting for minor party candidates are excluded from this table.

Source: Calculated from data provided by Bruce D. Bowen, C. Anthony Broh, and Charles L. Prysby, *Voting Behavior: The 1972 Election*, Supplementary Empirical Teaching Units in Political Science (Washington: American Political Science Association, 1975).

38

TABLE 2.9 Presidential and Congressional Vote by Party Identification, 1976

	Party Identification						
	Democratic			Independent	Republican		
	Strong	Weak	Independent	Independent	Independent	Weak	Strong
Presidential election: percent voting for							
Carter (D)	92	75	76	43	14	22	3
Ford (R)	8	25	24	57	86	78	97
	100	100	100	100	100	100	100
(N)	(270)	(374)	(186)	(172)	(174)	(250)	(201)
Congressional election: percent voting for							
Democratic Candidate	89	78	78	58	32	28	15
Republican Candidate	11	22	22	42	68	72	85
	100	100	100	100	100	100	100
(N)	(230)	(308)	(145)	(118)	(131)	(202)	(183)

Figures represent the percent voting for the specified candidate for each category of party identification. The number of respondents in the category is in parentheses. Nonvoters and those voting for minor party candidates are excluded, from this table.

Source: Calculated from data provided by Bruce D. Bowen, C. Anthony Broh, and Charles L. Prysby, *Voting Behavior: The 1976 Election*, Supplementary Empirical Teaching Units in Political Science (Washington: American Political Science Association, 1978).

with the increasing tendency of people to identify themselves in these terms, suggests a growing unpredictability and variability in election outcomes. Furthering this development is a change in the voting patterns of those with a partisan inclination; their tendency to vote for a presidential candidate of the opposite party has increased since the 1950s.[21]

Below the presidential level, party identification is more closely related to actual voting. For example, in 1972, when many Democrats voted for Nixon, congressional voting followed party lines: over 75 percent of the Democratic and Republican identifiers stayed with their party in the congressional balloting, while independents were split roughly 50–50 (see Table 2.8). In general, the less visible the office, the more voting falls along party lines. The reasons for this have to do with the information that voters possess about the issues and candidates. In low-visibility elections most voters usually know little about the candidates and thus are forced to rely on the party labels as cues for what the candidates stand for. Voting for a candidate of the opposite party occurs more often for presidential, senatorial, and gubernatorial elections, as these generally attract more media attention, and less often for such low-visibility offices as state representative or district judge.

Even below the presidential level, however, the relationship between party identification and voting has declined. This is evident in the rise of split ticket voting, shown in Figure 2.3. In recent elections, over half the voters have cast ballots for candidates of both parties. Furthermore, this ticket splitting is not simply a case of voters deviating at the presidential level and voting a straight ticket for all other offices. Almost all those who split their ballots do so below the presidential level as well.[22] Nor can this increased ticket splitting be fully accounted for by the rising number of independents, who naturally are less likely to vote a straight party ticket. Even among partisan identifiers, there is a greater tendency to vote a split ticket.[23] This diminished connection between party identification and voting behavior is symptomatic of the general decline in partisanship that has characterized American politics in the 1960s and 1970s.

Party identification is related also to the likelihood of voting. Strong partisans are the most likely to turn out on election day. Weak partisans and independent leaners have somewhat lower turnout rates, and pure independents are the least likely to cast a ballot. These patterns are evident in Table 2.10, which presents turnout rates for different categories of party identification. These differences in turnout mean that strong partisans are somewhat overrepresented among voters, while independents are slightly underrepresented.

The relationship of party identification to electoral participation is a result of its connection with psychological involvement in politics. The

Figure 2.3
SPLIT TICKET VOTING, 1960–1976.

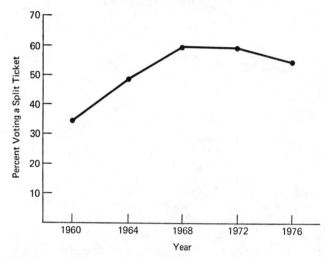

Source: Estimated from data in *The Gallup Opinion Index* (Princeton: Gallup International, 1976), Report No. 137, December 1976, p. 21; Norman H. Nie, Sidney Verba, and John R. Petrocik, *The Changing American Voter* (Cambridge: Harvard University Press, 1976), p. 53; and Everett Carll Ladd, Jr., with Charles D. Hadley, *Transformations of the American Party System: Political Coalitions from the New Deal to the 1970s.* (2nd ed. New York: Norton, 1978), p. 325. Where different figures for a specific year were reported by different sources, the estimate is an average of the reported data.

pure independents are the least interested in and concerned about elections, while strong partisans display the highest level of psychological involvement in partisan politics. Falling between these two extremes are the weak party identifiers and independent leaners, who are similar to each other in turnout. It also is clear that Republican identifiers and leaners have higher turnout rates than their Democratic counterparts, due largely to the higher educational levels of Republican supporters. These partisan differences in turnout mean that Republican attachments are somewhat more prevalent among voters than among the population as a whole.

Sources of Partisan Attachments

Partisan attachments tend to be formed relatively early in a person's life. By the time most individuals reach voting age, they have a basic awareness of the political parties and think of themselves as Democrats, Republicans, or independents. For some, the partisan attachments of adolescence or early adulthood may be only weak and unstable orientations, but for most they represent something more than that. The party

TABLE 2.10.   Turnout in the 1976 Presidential Election by Party Identification

Party Identification	Percent Voting	(N)
Strong Democrat	81	(339)
Weak ·Democrat	68	(538)
Independent Democrat	72	(280)
Independent	57	(342)
Independent Republican	74	(245)
Weak Republican	74	(254)
Strong Republican	92	(222)

The figures represent the percent of respondents in each category of party identification who claimed to have voted in the 1976 election. The numbers in parentheses indicate the total number of respondents in each category.

Source: Calculated from data provided by Bruce D. Bowen, C. Anthony Broh, and Charles L. Prysby, *Voting Behavior: The 1976 Election*, Supplementary Empirical Teaching Units in Political Science (Washington: American Political Science Association, 1978).

identification of an individual as he first enters the electorate is related to his partisan attachments later in life.

The initial formation of party identification is influenced by the individual's family. Young voters generally have a party identification that is congruent with that of their parents, at least in terms of being a Democrat, Republican, or independent. This generational transfer of partisan attachments is, of course, an imperfect one. The influence is the greatest when both parents have the same party identification (which is usually the case) and when the parents frequently discuss politics in the home.[24] When the parents fail to provide a consistent set of partisan cues, either because they differ or because they are apolitical, their influence on the party identifications of their children is less. Even when children do differ from their parents, it is unusual to find a completely opposite orientation. For example, when children with Democratic parents do not develop a Democratic identification, they usually think of themselves as independents, not as Republicans.[25]

Party identification also reflects the political milieu within which the individual first formed his partisan attachments. This means that current political events have a deeper impact on the partisan orientations of young people, for they are first establishing their party identifications. People of different age levels differ in their party identification not because growing older greatly affects partisan attitudes, but because they formed their party identifications in different political climate. The relevant fact about a person's age, in terms of its relationship to party identification, is that it indicates when the person grew up, not how many years the person has lived.

One example of the impact of political events on new voters involves the Great Depression. Our estimation of this impact necessarily is indirect. Information on party identification for the 1920s and 1930s is not directly available, as there was little survey research into electoral behavior at that time. Aggregate election statistics are available, of course, and they show a substantial shift to the Democrats in presidential and congressional voting, beginning in 1932. But these shifts in voting may not correspond to shifts in party identification. Many voters may have cast a ballot for Roosevelt yet retained an identification with the Republican Party. In order to examine partisan attachments we can look at the party identifications of respondents interviewed in election surveys during the 1950s.

The data reveal a clear pattern. Those who entered the electorate or grew up during the Great Depression were more Democratic in their party identification than older voters. Specifically, those born between 1910 and 1920 were distinctly more Democratic than those born between 1900 and 1910.[26] The difference is a generational one. Individuals born between 1910 and 1920 turned 21 between 1931 and 1941; they formed their partisan attachments during the Depression. Many older voters had formed a Republican identification prior to the Depression and, with an already established party identification, were less likely to identify as a Democrat in response to the events of the 1930s.

A less dramatic example of generational differences in party identification involves the declining partisanship of the 1960s and 1970s. As the data in Table 2.5 indicate, there has been a rise in the number of people identifying as independents. This is in large part a generational phenomenon. Younger members of the electorate, particularly those who entered the electorate after the early 1960s, are disproportionately likely to be independents.[27] The weak partisanship of younger voters is not due to age per se; those who entered the electorate in the 1950s were not so independent in orientation when they first attained voting age. Rather, it reflects a disenchantment with both major political parties, largely resulting from the political conflicts of the late 1960s and early 1970s. Older voters also were affected by the same phenomena, and their strength of partisanship has declined during the 1960s and 1970s.[28] But the impact of recent political events on the partisanship of older voters is less than for younger voters, producing a generational cleavage in party identification.

The partisan attachments of young voters understandably are affected by immediate political events. Many young voters are in the process of forming their party identification, and those who have formed one may not have firmly established it. Age differences in the stability of party identification are clearly illustrated by the results of a study that interviewed a national sample of high school seniors and their parents in 1965 and then reinterviewed the same people in 1973. About 40 percent of the 1965 high school seniors had changed their party identification (in terms of being a Democrat, Republican, or independent) by 1973. By contrast, less than one-fourth of their parents changed their party identification during that eight-year period.[29] Of course, during a period of greater political calm, both high school seniors and their parents might experience less change, but we would still expect greater stability from the older group.

Individuals alter their party identification in response to a variety of factors. In some cases, a change in party identification results from a change in personal circumstances. Getting married, taking a new job, or moving to a new community may expose an individual to new stimuli and produce new partisan orientations. One reason for the greater instability of party identification among young voters is the greater change they undergo in personal circumstances. Of course, changes due to personal factors will occur in all directions and will not tend to systematically benefit one party over the other. A more important source of change, in terms of its implications for the relative strength of the two parties, is an altered political environment. New social and economic conditions, new political problems, or new ways that the parties divide over issues may induce change in the partisan attachments of voters. The economic upheaval of the 1930s, for example, probably influenced some established Republicans to shift their partisan allegiances. In general, the political events that so strongly influence the partisan attachments of young voters also, to a lesser extent, affect party identifications among older voters.

In recent times, major shifts in party identification have taken place in the South. During the 1960s and 1970s there has been substantial change in the partisan attachments of white southerners, who once were extremely Democratic. The result has been a sizable increase in independents and a slight increase in Republican identifiers. Generational change, the replacement of old voters with new voters, accounts for some of this, but significant shifts have been registered by older white southerners.[30] This movement away from the Democratic Party appears to be a result of the political events of the 1960s. Conservative white southerners disagreed with the policies of the national Democratic Party, particularly with regard to racial and sociocultural issues, and responded by changing their partisan orientations. This is one example of how a change in political circumstances can produce a change in partisan attachments.

THE PSYCHOLOGICAL BASIS OF VOTING

The basic question about voting behavior is why people vote the way they do. Understanding the behavior of voters allows us to explain why a given election outcome occurred and to interpret the meaning of elections as a part of the political process. Unfortunately, this is a difficult task. Voters may have a variety of reasons for preferring one candidate without having a clear understanding of the exact role each factor plays in their decision. Moreover, voters may be unable to explain why they have certain perceptions of the candidates. The information obtained from sample surveys allows us to suggest some general tendencies, but it does not permit definitive statements.

Three basic reasons behind the voter's decision can be identified. The voter may prefer one candidate to the others on the basis of: (a) the public policy stands of the candidate; (b) the personal characteristics of the candidate; or (c) the party affiliation of the candidate. Similar reasons may be behind opposition to a particular candidate. One may vote against a candidate because of a dislike of the candidate's policy preferences, personal characteristics, or party ties. All three reasons may play a role in the voter's decision. The relative importance of each will vary from voter to voter. Some may cast their ballots more on the basis of the policy stands of the candidates, while others may be influenced primarily by the personal characteristics of the candidates. The role of each factor also varies among elections. For some offices in some years, voters may be guided largely by the party labels; in other cases, voters may make up their minds more on the basis of personal characteristics. Given that each factor plays an important role for some voters in some elections, we will examine each potential motive separately.

Policy Issues

The role of public policy issues in elections is of special interest to political analysts. Elections are widely viewed in democratic theory as providing a means for citizens to influence their government by selecting among contenders for office. The assumption is that the electorate will shape governmental policy by choosing candidates on the basis of what the candidates stand for. Where this does not appear to be the case, political observers often are quite critical. Indeed, many news commentators complained that Carter and Ford did not sufficiently address the issues during the 1976 presidential campaign. The term *issue* sometimes is used more generally to refer to anything that is a source of contention or conflict, but that is not its meaning here. Discussions of issue voting refer to the degree to which voters make up their minds on the basis of issues of public policy.

Public policy issues refer to questions of what the government should or should not do. Some policy issues in an election may be sharply defined, dealing with specific pieces of legislation or proposed programs. In 1976, for example, there were several specific issues, including the Equal Rights Amendment, the Panama Canal treaties, and a proposed constitutional amendment dealing with abortion. More often,

the policy issues are general, dealing with broad approaches to problems. Among such general policy issues in 1976 were questions of the
desirable tax reforms, whether we were going too far in the policy of
détente with Soviet Union, and the extent of federal government action
necessary to combat unemployment.

Two conditions must exist for a policy issue to directly influence the
candidate choices of voters: they must have an opinion on the issue and
they must perceive candidate differences on the issue. For any given
issue, many voters will fail to meet these conditions. Some will have no
opinion at all or one that is too weak and unstable to provide a basis for
evaluating the candidates. Among those who have a well-formed opinion on the issue, some will not see any difference between the candidates on the issue and thus will be unable to cast their ballots on this
basis. This inability to differentiate the candidate positions can exist
even for important issues and highly visible elections.

Where voters do have well-formed opinions and clear perceptions of
candidate differences, the potential for issue voting exists. On a given
issue, voters should be attracted to the candidate they feel to be closer
to their own position. Most voters are likely to be concerned about more
than one issue, however. A voter may see one candidate as better
representing his preferences on some issues and the other candidate as
better representing his preferences on other issues, thus complicating
the decision. In such cases, the voter presumably would have to decide
which candidate he was closer to in general. What really should matter
is how the voter perceives the positions of the candidates in relation to
his own attitudes. Where the voter feels he is closer to one of the
candidates on the issues, he should be more likely to vote for that
candidate. Such feelings naturally depend upon two critical factors: (a)
which issues the voter sees as important; and (b) what the voter thinks
the candidates stand for.

The role of the Vietnam War issue in the 1968 presidential election
is a good illustration of several aspects of issue voting. The war certainly
was an important issue to most voters in 1968, and it would have been
reasonable to expect that feelings about the war would be a prime
determinant of the vote. The data in Table 2.11, however, indicate that
orientations on the war were only weakly related to presidential voting.
The explanation for this has to do with perceptions of candidate
stands.[31] Many voters were unable to see any difference between Nixon
and Humphrey. Furthermore, there was little consensus among those
who did see differences between the two major candidates; some saw
Nixon as more dovish while others saw him as more hawkish. Voters had
far less difficulty in placing Wallace; he was widely seen as definitely
hawkish and drew most of his votes from the pro-war segments of the
population. It may be that an inability to clearly differentiate Nixon and

TABLE 2.11   Presidential Vote by Vietnam War Orientation, 1968

Presidential Vote	Vietnam War Orientation		
	Withdrawal	Mixed View	Military Victory
Nixon	43	50	47
Humphrey	51	44	31
Wallace	6	6	22
	100	100	100
(N)	(195)	(475)	(273)

Respondents were asked to place themselves on a seven-point scale running from immediate withdrawal to complete military victory. For ease of analysis, this seven-point scale was collapsed to three categories. The above figures indicate the precent of respondents in each opinion category voting for each presidential candidate. Those not voting, voting for minor candidates, or not expressing an opinion on this issue are excluded from this table.

Source: 1968 election survey conducted by the Survey Research Center, University of Michigan.

Humphrey was an appropriate response to the ambiguity of the two candidates on the issue, but it does illustrate the difficulties that voters may face in attempting to base their vote on questions of public policy.

Four years later, the Vietnam War issue played a different role in the presidential election. As the data in Table 2.12 show, the orientations of voters on that issue were strongly related to their vote. Most voters had little difficulty in seeing McGovern as more dovish than Nixon, and while some voters were attracted to McGovern on this basis, most were not. Only about 30 percent of the voters felt that McGovern was closer to their point of view on the war.[32] The contrast between the impact

TABLE 2.12   Presidential Vote by Vietnam War Orientation, 1972

Presidential Vote	Vietnam War Orientation		
	Withdrawal	Mixed View	Military Victory
Nixon	34	74	87
McGovern	66	26	13
	100	100	100
(N)	(438)	(783)	(268)

Respondents were asked to place themselves on a seven-point scale running from immediate withdrawal to complete military victory. For ease of analysis, this seven-point scale was collapsed to three categories. The above figures indicate the precent of respondents in each opinion category voting for each presidential candidate. Those not voting, voting for minor candidates, or not expressing an opinion on this issue are excluded from this table.

Source: Calculated from data provided by Bruce D. Bowen, C. Anthony Broh, and Charles L. Prysby, Voting Behavior: The 1972 Election, Supplementary Empirical Teaching Units in Political Science (Washington: American Political Science Association, 1975).

of the war issue in the 1968 and 1972 elections suggests that the extent of issue voting is dependent on the electoral context. When the candidates take clear and distinct stands on major issues, the extent of issue voting may be relatively high. When they do not, issue voting will be low.

Voters also may be influenced by their perceptions of the general liberal or conservative nature of the candidates. Few voters are ideological in a strict sense of the term, but most willingly classify themselves in liberal or conservative terms. Furthermore, their classification does correspond, albeit imperfectly, to their positions on specific issues. In evaluating the candidates in an election, voters may form impressions of the general liberal or conservative orientation of each candidate and react accordingly. In cases where the candidates are seen as ideologically distinct, voting patterns should reflect this.

The 1972 presidential election is an example of clear ideological differences between the candidates. If we divide the voters into liberals, moderates, and conservatives, on the basis of their self-classification, we find that these ideological groups differed considerably in their vote (see Table 2.13). Voters generally saw McGovern as quite liberal and Nixon as moderately conservative, and the election results reveal this.

TABLE 2.13 Presidential Vote in the 1972 and 1976 Elections by Ideological Orientation

	Ideological Orientation		
Presidential Vote	Liberal	Moderate	Conservative
1972			
Nixon	31	69	87
McGovern	69	31	13
	100	100	100
(*N*)	(318)	(421)	(453)
1976			
Carter	78	52	22
Ford	22	48	78
	100	100	100
(*N*)	(295)	(434)	(503)

The percentage figures indicate the presidential choices of major party voters according to their ideological self-classification. Those not voting, voting for a minor party candidate, or not expressing an ideological orientation are excluded from this table.

Source: Calculated from data provided by Bruce D. Bowen, C. Anthony Broh, and Charles L. Prysby, *Voting Behavior: The 1976 Election*, Supplementary Empirical Teaching Units in Political Science (Washington: American Political Science Association, 1978) and from data provided by Bruce D. Bowen, C. Anthony Broh, and Charles L. Prysby, *Voting Behavior: The 1972 Election*, Supplementary Empirical Teaching Units in Political Science (Washington: American Political Science Association, 1975).

Given the number of moderates and conservatives, only a minority of voters perceived themselves as ideologically closer to McGovern, so the overall impact of this dimension worked to Nixon's advantage.

In 1976 voters did not have such distinct perceptions of the ideological nature of the two presidential candidates. Carter, for example, was seen as a liberal by some, as a moderate by others, and even as a conservative by a few. On the whole, Carter was seen as moderately liberal and Ford as moderately conservative, but the difference between the two major candidates was less than in 1972.[33] Even so, the data in Table 2.13 indicates that liberal, moderate, and conservative voters differed greatly in their presidential choice in 1976. Although few voters saw either candidate as ideologically extreme, most apparently perceived enough difference for this consideration to enter into their vote decision. Thus, even in cases where the candidates are perceived in moderate terms, voters may cast their ballots, at least in part, on the basis of their perceptions of the general liberal or conservative nature of the candidates.

Overall, the extent of issue voting appears to have increased during the 1960s and 1970s. There is some controversy over the amount of change that has taken place, but several pieces of evidence suggest that the electorate is more issue-oriented and more ideological now than it was during the 1950s. The differences are clearest for presidential elections. When asked what they liked and disliked about the presidential candidates, only about one-half of the electorate made any reference to issues in 1956 or 1960; in subsequent presidential elections about 70 percent of the electorate evaluated the candidate in terms of issues.[34] Similarly, the correlation between issue orientations and the direction of the vote increased during the 1960s.[35] Also, voters in the 1960s and 1970s more often referred to general ideological terms as reasons for liking or disliking the presidential candidates than was the case in the 1950s.[36] These developments are due largely to the changed nature of electoral politics. As we shall see in the next chapter, the types of issues and the nature of candidate behavior that characterized the 1960s and 1970s made for a different electoral environment.

Personal Characteristics of Candidates

Voters judge candidates by their personal characteristics as well as by their issue stands. Included among the relevant personal characteristics would be such things as the intelligence, sincerity, honesty, and competence of the candidates. Quite apart from how they see the candidates on the issues, voters form images of the qualifications and abilities of the candidates. In fact, the perception of the personal attributes of the candidates probably is the most important influence on the vote.

Perceptions of the personal characteristics of the candidates are not independent of the evaluations of the issue positions of the candidates. It certainly would be difficult for a voter to see a candidate as intelligent and competent if the candidate favors policies that are anathema to the voter. The influence may operate in the opposite direction as well. Voters having a favorable image of a candidate's personal characteristics may tend to adopt some of the positions put forth by the candidate or to misperceive what policies the candidate stands for, in order to create greater similarity between their perception of the candidate's policy positions and their own preferences. Still, there will be many cases where these two dimensions of candidate evaluation do not correspond so well, and voters are just as likely to vote for the candidate with the more desirable personal attributes, as they see them, as for the candidate with the better policy positions.

The role of perceived candidate attributes in recent presidential elections illustrates the above points. McGovern did poorly not only because of voter disagreement with his policy positions, but also because he was negatively perceived in personal terms. When asked what they liked and disliked about the presidential candidates, respondents in the University of Michigan's 1972 election survey frequently identified negative aspects of McGovern's personality. The most cited criticisms of McGovern were insincerity, inability to keep promises, indecisiveness, impracticality, and being too negative. In contrast, Nixon generally was perceived in favorable terms, with experience being the personal attribute most often mentioned.[37]

Evaluations of personal attributes did not work so greatly to the advantage of one candidate in the 1976 presidential election. Positive and negative views of Carter and Ford were voiced, with both candidates basically being positively rated. Ford appears to have been seen in slightly more favorable terms with regard to personal characteristics, but the differences were small compared to recent presidential elections. One preelection poll found that registered voters were fairly even in their ratings of the intelligence, leadership ability, and sincerity of the candidates. Carter was seen by more respondents as being concerned about people and their problems, but he also was more often seen as "wishy-washy." Ford received higher marks on knowledge about the government, which was a natural consequence of his greater experience at the national level. The closeness of the election reflects in part the fact that neither candidate was able to convince the electorate that he had superior personal qualities for being president.[38]

Personal characteristics of the candidates are equally important in subpresidential elections. Senators, governors, and congressmen are often elected and reelected because the voters have favorable images of their personal characteristics. Perceptions of the experience, competence, and leadership abilities of candidates greatly influence how people cast their ballots for such offices as senator or governor.[39] And for many less visible state and local offices, the only information that many voters will have about most candidates will be about the personal characteristics of the candidates.

Voters rely heavily on perceptions of candidate attributes for several reasons. First, they may not see any crucial differences in the policy stands of the candidates. This situation often is a result of the campaign methods and themes employed by the candidates, as they frequently prefer to appeal to the electorate by endorsing broad goals and avoiding specific policy committments. Many voters in many elections may feel that the significant differences between the candidates are their personal characteristics, not their policy stands. Moreover, political problems are often complex, and the voter may lack the expertise necessary to evaluate proposed solutions. Thus, an awareness of differences in the policies candidates propose may not help the voter to choose between the candidates. In general, it is easier for voters to form impressions of the personal attributes of candidates than to understand and evaluate the differences in the policy stands of the candidates. This is particularly true for elections to the lower-level offices, as less information about the candidates usually is available. The reliance of voters on perceptions of personal characteristics, then, is a result of both the type of information available to the voter and the voter's ability to handle different types of information.

The importance that voters place on candidate attributes is criticized by some observers, who see this as basing the vote decison on the wrong types of factors. This may be true in some cases; no doubt some voters are greatly influenced by such things as the candidate's physical appearance, manner of speaking, age, sex, or race, all of which probably are irrelevant to how the candidate would perform in office. For the most part, however, voters refer to personal attributes that are more directly related to behavior in public office. The impressions that the voter has of various leadership-related characteristics, such as competence or sincerity, are relevant considerations. If a voter sees a candidate as incompetent or untrustworthy, it makes no sense for the voter to cast his ballot for that candidate, regardless of how much the voter agrees with the policy statements of the candidate.

Party Ties

Rather than choosing among candidates on the basis of their personal characteristics or policy positons, a voter may cast his ballot for a candidate because of the candidate's political party affiliation. This is not possible in nonpartisan or primary elections, for there are no party labels to guide the voters in these cases, but the voters may respond to the candidates in partisan general elections in terms of whether they are Democrats or Republicans. The party label a candidate runs under therefore affects how voters respond to him and influences his chance of being elected.

The simplest form of influence of party labels on the vote decision occurs when a voter casts his ballot on the basis of his party identification. Most voters express some attachment to one of the two major parties (pure independents comprise only about 15 percent of the electorate). These attachments indicate assessments of the two parties, and they provide useful guides to the voters. If a voter feels that one party better represents his political interests and goals, then he will probably vote for the candidate of the party he prefers, unless there are countervailing reasons. Such reasons may come from specific information about the candidates. A voter who identifies with one party may support the candidate of the other party because he finds that candidate's personal attributes or policy stands more attractive. But where little or no information about the candidates is readily available, which often is the case in elections for lower-level offices, voters will lack reasons to vote against their party identification.

The influence of party attachments on voting behavior reflects in large part a political orientation that focuses on questions of group interest. People often think about politics in terms of which groups benefit from government actions, and such views permit long-lasting orientations. The specific political issues of greatest concern change as time passes, but the more general questions of group benefits and group conflict remain. Furthermore, voters generally are able to differentiate the parties along group lines. For many reasons, voters develop images of the parties that refer to the types of groups the parties represent or favor. The Democrats generally have been seen as representing the working class, trade unions, and minority groups, whereas the Republicans generally are viewed as favoring business groups and the upper middle class. These images of the parties provide a basis for voting when little is known about the candidates in a specific election. A trade union member may vote for the Democratic candidate in a state legislative election simply because he feels the Democratic Party is better for the working man. A lawyer may vote Republican in the same election on the grounds that the Republican Party better represents his economic interests.

Party labels can affect voting behavior in another way. Specific political events may lead individuals to vote Democratic or Republican, regardless of their party identification. Some contemporary presidential elections provide examples of this possibility. Roosevelt's victory over Hoover in 1932 was largely a result of voter repudiation of the Hoover administration. Regardless of whom the Democrats nominated, their candidate would have started the campaign with a sizable advantage, due to the economic collapse that occurred during Hoover's first term. Similarly, Eisenhower's election in 1952 reflected voter dissatisfaction with the Truman administration. Although Truman was not running in 1952, the Democratic presidential candidate, Stevenson, suffered as a result of the desire of some voters to punish the Democrats. More recently, Ford had to deal with the disadvantage of being a Republican in 1976. Although not personally involved in the Watergate scandals, Ford nevertheless was hurt by being a part of the same party as Nixon. In general, voters may react to the performance of the party in power and vote accordingly in the next election. Thus, even when a voter casts a ballot that differs from his partisan attachment, the primary motives behind the vote may be general reactions to the parties, not evaluations of the characteristics and positions of the candidates.

The 1976 presidential election offers another example of how events may affect voter reactions to party labels. High rates of unemployment and inflation during Ford's administration led to considerable dissatisfaction with economic conditions. While not everyone blamed Ford for the economic situation, many voters undoubtedly felt that a change of administrations was called for. Table 2.14 shows that voters who felt the government had been doing a poor job of handling the economy were extremely likely to vote for Carter. Those who felt that the government's economic policy had been good (a less popular opinion) voted heavily for Ford.

TABLE 2.14   Presidential Vote by Opinion of Government Economic Policy, 1976

	Opinion of Economic Policy		
Presidential Vote	Good	Fair	Poor
Carter	27	54	73
Ford	73	46	27
	100	100	100
(N)	(178)	(987)	(434)

Figures indicate the precent of respondents in each opinion category voting for Carter or Ford. The number of respondents in each category is in parentheses. Respondents not voting or voting for a minor candidate are excluded from this table.

Source: Calculated from data provided by Bruce D. Bowen, C. Anthony Broh, and Charles L. Prysby, *Voting Behavior: The 1976 Election*, Supplementary Empirical Teaching Units in Political Science (Washington: American Political Science Association, 1978).

This relationship between presidential vote and opinion of the government's economic policy involves more than just a simple rejection of a Republican administration because of hard times, however. Even those who were critical of the government's economic policy might not have voted for Carter if they thought that he would do no better. Thus, questions of Carter's personal competence and capabilities were relevant factors here as well. Similarly, some voters may have been disturbed by the kinds of economic policies that they thought Carter would try to implement. This example is a case where questions of public policy and candidate characteristics interacted with partisan images to determine how voters responded to the economic conditions preceding the 1976 election.

Elections are often in part a referendum on the performance of the incumbent administration. Voters in 1976 cast their ballots partially on the basis of their feelings about the previous Republican administrations. Similarly, the landslide Republican presidential vote in 1972 owed something to the fact that many people felt positively about the first Nixon administration. The same phenomenon can occur below the presidential level as well. Voters in a state election, for example, might shift toward the Republican candidates in reaction to the performance of the incumbent Democratic governor.

The three factors affecting the vote—issues of public policy, evaluations of the candidates' characteristics, and reactions to the parties— are interrelated aspects of electoral politics. In the short run these factors are tied together because the particular candidates and issues involved in an election have obvious partisan ties. There are long-run connections as well. Parties develop images of what they stand for, and these images affect voting behavior. The next chapter will discuss these long-run factors in more detail.

FOR FURTHER READING

A good discussion of registration laws and their impact on voting is in William J. Crotty, *Political Reform and the American Experiment.*[40] Sidney Verba and Norman Nie, *Participation in America,*[41] examine the social and psychological sources of voting as well as other forms of political participation. The concept of party identification is discussed in Angus Campbell et al., *The American Voter,*[42] which also looks at the psychological basis of the vote. The decline of partisanship and the rise of issue voting are analyzed by Norman Nie, Sidney Verba, and John Petrocik, *The Changing American Voter.*[43] An interesting examination of voter behavior in presidential elections is *The Responsible Electorate,* by V. O. Key, Jr.[44]

NOTES

1. *Election Administration Reports,* Vol. 7, No. 1 (January 5, 1977), p. 2.

2. Center for Political Studies, *The CPS 1976 American National Election Study*, Vol. 1 (Ann Arbor, Mich.: Inter-University Consortium for Political and Social Research, 1977), p. 332.

3. *Election Administration Reports,* Vol. 7, No. 1 (January 5, 1977), p. 2; Raymond Wolfinger and Steven Rosenstone, "Who Votes?" (Paper presented at the 1977 annual meeting of the American Political Science Association, Washington, D.C., September 1–4, 1977), p. 13.

4. Richard F. Yalch, "Pre-election Interview Effects on Voter Turnout." *Public Opinion Quarterly,* Vol. 40, No. 3 (Fall 1976), pp. 331–336.

5. Wolfinger and Rosenstone, "Who Votes?" p. 48.

6. U.S. Bureau of the Census, *The Statistical Abstract of the United States:1976,* 97th edition (Washington, D.C.: U.S. Government Printing Office, 1976), p. 467.

7. North Dakota does not have voter registration. Some states do not require registration for those in rural areas.

8. William J. Crotty, *Political Reform and the American Experiment* (New York: Crowell, 1977), p. 38.

9. Stanley Kelley, Jr., Richard E. Ayres, and William G. Bowen, "Registration and Voting: Putting First Things First," *American Political Science Review,* Vol. 61, No. 2 (June 1967), p. 362.

10. Ibid., pp. 373–374.

11. Steven J. Rosenstone and Raymond E. Wolfinger, "The Effect of Registration Laws on Voter Turnout," *American Political Science Review,* Vol. 72, No. 1 (March 1978), p. 35.

12. Ibid., p. 33.

13. Angus Campbell et al., *The American Voter* (New York: Wiley, 1960), pp. 101–103.

14. Ibid., p. 104.

15. Herbert Asher, *Presidential Elections and American Politics* (Homewood, Ill.: Dorsey, 1976), p. 8.

16. Campbell et al., *The American Voter,* pp. 105–106.

17. Some analysts have asked why anyone bothers to vote at all, given the extremely low likelihood of any voter affecting the election outcome. For example, see Anthony Downs, *An Economic Theory of Democracy* (New York: Harper 1957), pp. 260–276. In this sense, voting is not a "rational act" and our study of it must realize that fact.

18. Lester W. Milbrath and M. L. Goel, *Political Participation* (2nd ed.; Skokie, Ill.: Rand McNally, 1977), p. 120.

19. Older people also are likely to have lower levels of education, which contributes to their decreased likelihood of voting.

20. Center for Political Studies, *The CPS 1976 American National Election Study*, pp. 72–76.

21. Norman H. Nie, Sidney Verba, and John R. Petrocik, *The Changing American Voter* (Cambridge, Mass.: Harvard University, 1976), p. 51.

22. Ibid., p. 53.

23. Ibid., p. 51.

24. M. Kent Jennings and Richard G. Niemi, *The Political Character of Adolescence* (Princeton, N.J.: Princeton University, 1974), p. 54.

25. Ibid., pp. 39–41.

26. Campbell et al., *The American Voter*, p. 154.

27. Nie, Verba, and Petrocik, *The Changing American Voter*, p. 63.

28. Ibid.

29. Richard G. Niemi and Herbert Weisberg, *Controversies in American Voting Behavior* (San Francisco: Freeman, 1976), p. 308.

30. Paul Allen Beck, "Partisan Dealignment in the Postwar South," *American Political Science Review*, Vol. 71, No. 2 (June 1977), p. 485.

31. Benjamin I. Page and Richard A. Brody, "Policy Voting and the Electoral Process: The Vietnam War Issue," *American Political Science Review*, Vol. 66, No. 3 (September 1972), pp. 979–995.

32. Arthur H. Miller et al., "A Majority Party in Disarray: Policy Polarization in the 1972 Election," *American Political Science Review*, Vol. 70, No. 3 (September 1976), p. 759.

33. Arthur H. Miller and Warren E. Miller, "Partisanship and Performance: 'Rational' Choice in the 1976 Presidential Elections" (Paper presented at the 1977 annual meeting of the American Political Science Association, Washington, D.C., September 1–4, 1977), p. 57.

34. Nie, Verba, and Petrocik, *The Changing American Voter*, p. 167.

35. Ibid., p. 165.

36. Ibid., p. 113.

37. David E. RePass, "Comment," *American Political Science Review,* Vol. 70, No. 3 (September 1976), p. 822.

38. Miller and Miller, "Partisanship and Performance," pp. 89–99.

39. Gerald D. Wright, Jr., *Electoral Choice in America* (Chapel Hill, N.C.: Institute for Research in Social Science, 1974), p. 66.

40. New York: Crowell, 1977.

41. New York. Harper, 1972.

42. New York: Wiley, 1960.

43. Cambridge, Mass.: Harvard University, 1976.

44. Cambridge, Mass.: Harvard University, 1966.

CHAPTER 3

Parties, Issues, and Social Groups

Electoral competiton in the United States takes place within the context of a two-party system. The serious candidates almost always are Democrats or Republicans. The voters also think in terms of a two-party system, with the vast majority expressing some attachment to either the Democratic or the Republican party. The previous chapter has discussed the nature of party identification and its effect on how people vote. Clearly the electorate's images of and loyalties to the two major political parties constitute important aspects of electoral politics. This chapter further examines these electoral parameters, including how they have been altered over the past several decades. Two major topics are of concern here. First, we need to outline the policy differences between the two parties, at least as they are perceived by the electorate. In other words, what do voters see as the significant differences between Democrats and Republicans? Second, we wish to examine the ties between political parties and social groups; put simply, what types of people does each party tend to appeal to? Since the fundamental differences between the two parties have been shaped by the realignment of the 1930s, we shall take that as our starting point.

THE REALIGNMENT OF THE 1930S

The last critical realignment of the American political party system occurred in the 1930s. A critical realignment refers to a relatively rapid, fundamental, and durable alteration in the pattern of party loyalties.[1]

Such realignments occur infrequently. Before the realignment of the 1930s, realignments occurred in the 1850s and the 1890s. Of course, in any time period there is some alteration in the party attachments of the electorate, but only rarely is the change substantial enough to qualify as a realignment.

The General Nature of Realignment

Critical realignments involve three elements. The most important feature is a redefinition of the cleavage between the two parties. New points of disagreement emerge or are made sharper, so that the basic differences between the parties are fundamentally redrawn. As a consequence of this change, a second feature of a major realignment usually emerges: the social base of support for each party is reshaped. Social and demographic characteristics relate to voting patterns after a realignment in a way different from the prerealignment pattern. A final aspect of a realignment, although not a necessary one, is a substantial change in the party balance. The changes in the political and social character of the two parties probably will result in changes in the degree of support they can command among the electorate. The shifts in party strength may be enough to cause the former minority party to become the majority party. An even more radical alteration in the party balance occurs when a new political party emerges and/or one of the old parties breaks up. This was the case in 1850s, as the Republican Party emerged while the Whig Party died.

Drawing upon the nature of past realignments, we can sketch out the general development of a realignment. The starting point is the emergence of new political issues, often related together as part of a basic political problem. To many voters, these issues must be of great concern, important enough to break apart existing partisan loyalties. Moreover, the new issues must generate substantial conflict. That is, the population must be divided in its opinions, not in agreement on how to handle the new problems.

The impact of these new dimensions of political conflict on the party system depends on two variables: how the parties respond to the new issues and how the cleavages over the new issues correspond to the old party divisions.[2] Significant impact occurs when the two parties divide clearly and when the new cleavage line cuts across the old party lines. The likely result in such a situation is an upheaval in party loyalties, with the party dissidents moving over to the party they agree with on the new issues. But the parties may not divide so clearly, or the new cleavage lines may correspond to the old party divisions. In such cases, substantial change in the party system may not occur. A variety of other possibilities exist, including the emergence of a new political party and the breakup of one of the old parties. Perhaps the greatest possible change would be the disappearance of the existing parties and replacement by new ones.

Regardless of the form it takes, realignment involves a substantial and lasting change in the party system. This change is usually understood to be fairly rapid, with a particular election identified as the critical one. While the changes may seem centered in a brief time period, the beginnings of the realignment often can be placed somewhat earlier and the realignment may not be completed until much later. It also is possible for fundamental alterations in the party system to occur as a result of a series of comparatively minor shifts and developments. In such a case, the change during any brief time period would be small, but the cumulative impact over a long period of time would be great. The term *secular realignment* is used to distinguish this type of realignment from the more dramatic *critical realignment*.[3] The difference between the two is in the pace of change, not in the amount of change or its durability.

The New Deal Realignment

The realignment of the 1930s provides an excellent example of the realignment process. Before 1932 the Republicans were the majority party, this dominant position having been established in the realignment of the 1890s. Republican presidential candidates easily won the 1920, 1924, and 1928 presidential elections, and Republicans outpolled Democrats in congressional elections throughout the 1920s. The Democrats were extremely strong in the South, due to the strong anti-Republican feelings among white southerners that resulted from the Civil War and Reconstruction, but elsewhere the Republicans dominated. The disparities in party strength did not correspond to differences in what the parties stood for. Both parties had progressive and conservative elements, but overall differences were small, and a similar probusiness orientation characterized the leadership of both parties. All of this was changed during the 1930s. The Democrats became the majority party and established control of the White House and the Capitol. Along with the shifts in the party balance, considerable differences between the two major parties developed. These differences between the parties have remained with us, although in a diluted form, to the present time.

The immediate cause of the New Deal realignment was the Great Depression. The economic chaos that began during Herbert Hoover's first year in the White House steadily worsened to the point where one-fourth of the labor force was unemployed by the end of his term. This alone would in all likelihood have caused Hoover to be defeated. But a defeat of Hoover and a blaming of the Republicans for the economic problems would not imply realignment. Other important developments were necessary. Particularly important was the way the two parties responded to the depression.

The first years of the Great Depression generated conflict over the appropriate government action. Conservatives preached caution and restraint, claiming that the proper role of the federal government was a limited one. Economic forces needed to work themselves out, it was argued, and excessive government interference was unwise. The liberal position was that the federal government needed to act decisively to pull the country out of the depression. Additionally, liberals argued that the federal government had to help with the relief problems stemming from massive unemployment. Conservatives, on the other hand, took the position that the relief problem should be handled by the state and local governments.[4]

Both parties had liberal and conservative spokesmen, but during Hoover's first term these two orientations became associated with the two major parties. The Republicans placed themselves squarely on the conservative side of social and economic questions. Hoover was renominated in 1932, and he and his party continued to resist drastic federal government action. The Democrats, on the other hand, moved toward the liberal end of the spectrum. To be sure, this was a slow and cautious movement. Even the Democratic nominee in 1932, Franklin D. Roosevelt, avoided radical proposals in his campaign. But during Hoover's first administration, the Democratic Party had committed itself to supporting an active role for the federal government.[5]

Once Roosevelt took office the differences between the parties began to sharpen. A flood of legislation was passed during Roosevelt's first administration, expanding the social and economic activities of the federal government severalfold. Republicans by and large were critical of Roosevelt's programs. By 1936 there was no doubt that the two parties stood for different things—the Democrats for an active and expanded federal government and the Republicans for limited government and nonintervention in social and economic matters.

The Great Depression was the catalyst for the New Deal realignment. Yet behind this specific event were more general issues that had been developing throughout the twentieth century. These issues were related to the economic development of the U.S. As the country became more industrialized and more urbanized, new problems became important, including those concerning labor–management relations, adequate housing and social conditions in the cities, and the equitable distribution of the national income. Moreover, the ranks of the urban working class were often filled by immigrants or first-generation Americans, as some 19 million people entered the country between 1900 and 1930.[6] This introduced another political problem: coping with discrimination against many ethnic groups and integrating these elements into American life. Because the Depression hit the poorer and less-established groups the hardest, it made many of the above problems more acute. The result was that conflict over economic issues in the 1930s was in part conflict over how to deal with the Depression and in part conflict over the more general nature of social and economic policy.

The New Deal Coalition

The realignment of the 1930s transformed the Democrats into the majority party. The basis of this majority was the New Deal coalition forged by Roosevelt. The New Deal coalition combined support from the working class and various ethnic and minority groups with the already established strength in the South. This broad coalition provided the electoral support that allowed the Democrats to dominate national politics during the Roosevelt administration.

The introduction of class cleavages into the American party system was the most important aspect of the New Deal era. Some class differences probably existed before 1932, but they were slight. By 1936 significant class differences had been established. Those in the working class—manual laborers and blue-collar industrial workers—disproportionately voted Democratic. Middle class voters—professionals, managers, and white-collar employees—were relatively more Republican in their sympathies (although Roosevelt did well even among these groups). During the 1930s, strong ties between labor unions and the Democratic Party were established. Corresponding connections between the Republicans and many business groups became an equally important feature of the political landscape. These group ties and voting patterns were reflected in the popular images of the two parties. The Democrats were seen as the party of the working man and the economically disadvantaged—what Roosevelt referred to as the "forgotten man." The Republican Party, by contrast, was identified as the party of big business, upper-income groups, and the middle class.

The New Deal also had a strong ethnocultural character. European immigrants and first-generation Americans were becoming a force in American politics, and they leaned very much in the Democratic direction. Democratic orientations among ethnic groups in part reflected the concentration of these groups within the working class, but more than social class was involved. The Democrats appealed to the disadvantaged and less–established groups within the society, and this often was defined in ethnic or cultural terms, with the Protestant–Catholic distinction providing a rough indication of this dimension. Historically, the Democrats had received substantial Catholic support, and when they nominated Al Smith, a Catholic, as their presidential candidate in 1928, their support from various ethnic groups was strengthened. These tendencies were further solidified under Roosevelt, as evidenced by the fact that over 80 percent of white Catholics voted for him in 1936.[7]

Democratic tendencies among working-class and ethnic groups were a feature of northern politics. In the South, the Democrats simply remained the dominant party, as they had been for decades prior to the New Deal realignment. Ethnic cleavages were not a feature of southern electoral behavior. Blacks were excluded from voting for the most part, and other minority ethnic and religious groups were extremely small, so the result was an electorate composed basically of white Anglo-Saxon Protestants. Class cleavages also were absent in the South. White middle-class southerners were as Democratic as their working-class counterparts.[8]

The New Deal coalition can be described in terms of issue orientations as well as social characteristics. The basic division between the Democratic and Republican parties concerned the role of the federal government in domestic social and economic matters. Besides favoring vigorous action to combat the economic problems of the 1930s, the Democrats endorsed an expanded role for the national government in general. This implied, among other things, government interference in the economy through the use of fiscal and monetary policy and more thorough regulation of private enterprise. Along with greater interference in and control over the economy, the Roosevelt program stressed another type of socioeconomic activism: federal government sponsorship of a variety of social-welfare measures. These policies, such as unemployment insurance or the Social Security system, were designed to reduce the burden of economic misfortune and to provide a measure of social equality.

Not all Democrats favored Roosevelt's policies. In fact, the 1924 and 1928 Democratic presidential nominees, John Davis and Al Smith, were against the New Deal programs.[9] Nor did all Republicans oppose these policies. The realignment of the 1930s involved shifts and changes within and between the parties that were not worked out immediately, and some diversity remained in each party. But by the end of the 1930s the two parties had developed distinct orientations on social and economic issues. To a great extent, the contemporary meaning of the terms *liberal* and *conservative* is based on these differences. The Democratic Party, favoring federal government economic activism and social-welfare policies to benefit the economically disadvantaged, was the liberal party. The Republican Party, emphasizing the benefits of limited government and a reliance on the free market, was the conservative party. To be sure, other elements can be considered part of the liberal–conservative dimension, and some aspects of the meaning of these terms have changed over time, but the core element remains.

In sum, the New Deal coalition transformed the Democrats into the majority party. Working-class and ethnic group support in the North was added to the already solidly Democratic South. The basis of this coalition was the New Deal program of the Roosevelt administration. When it came to domestic social and economic issues, the Democrats and Republicans were clearly differentiated along liberal and conservative lines, at least at the national level. All these characteristics of the party system have remained to some extent, but there have been many changes. One way of looking at electoral politics over the past few decades is in terms of the changes in—or breakup of—the New Deal coalition. The remainder of this chapter will do just that, first by examining changes in the way that social characteristics are tied to partisan choice, then by analyzing the changes in the way that ideological and issue orientations relate to voting behavior.

SOCIAL FACTORS AND VOTING BEHAVIOR

We commonly think of political candidates as appealing more to some social groups than to others. Political commentators often speak of the black vote, the union vote, the youth vote, and so on. Any analysis of voting data reveals that while the various social groups by no means vote as a bloc, there are appreciable differences along these lines. Some groups are relatively more Democratic in their voting patterns, while others are disproportionately Republican. These differences exist for several reasons. First, different social groups naturally have different political interests and goals, and in any election one candidate may support these interests and goals more than the other candidates. Also, historical tendencies for one party to support the demands of a group tend to reinforce and perpetuate themselves as voters develop certain images of the parties. The relationship between parties and groups may be strengthened by organizational ties, particularly where the leaders of a group organization actively support and campaign for a candidate. Finally, a candidate may appeal to a group simply because he is a member of the group.

This brief outline of the reasons for group differences in partisan tendencies suggests why the relationships between social factors and voting behavior change over time. The political interests and goals of a group may change, either because of changes in the group or because of changes in the political environment. Groups may move away from one party and toward the other because the parties change; the party that once supported the demands of a group may move in a different direction. As time passes, the images of the parties may be altered, perhaps for some of the above reasons, leading to more change. Naturally, these factors are interrelated. Changes in the importance of various issues, the nature of group demands, and the way the parties respond often are part of some broader process of change.

The three most important social characteristics that affect voting behavior are: (a) social class or socioeconomic position; (b) ethnicity, including race and religion, which is linked to ethnicity in the American context; and (c) region, particularly the North–South division. These three factors are themselves interrelated, but each exercises a separate effect on voting. Other social characteristics are far less important, often being related to partisan choice primarily because of a relationship with these three important characteristics.

Social Class and Partisan Choice

As previous sections emphasized, the New Deal realignment introduced significant class cleavages into American electoral politics, creating images of the Democrats and Republicans as the parties of the working class and middle class, respectively. We would like to know, however, how much difference in voting behavior actually exists between different social classes. Additionally, class cleavages are not likely to be constant, so it is useful to determine the conditions or circumstances that lead to greater class distinctiveness in voting behavior. Put simply, for what groups, and in what situations, is social class electorally relevant, and what tendencies appear to be emerging?

Our use of the term *social class* is broad. Analysts of social stratification distinguish between social class, socioeconomic status, and economic position. We shall treat these as referring to the same general phenomenon. The existence of class differences implies two basic socioeconomic features: (a) individuals differ with respect to their position in the system of production and distribution of goods and services; and (b) individuals differ with respect to being economically advantaged or disadvantaged. Because of these features of the socioeconomic system, groups differ in their economic interests, which leads to political differences.

The degree to which social class is related to voting behavior will depend on how social class is defined and measured. One common method is to use occupation and focus on the distinction between manual and nonmanual workers. Manual, or blue-collar, workers are considered working class, while nonmanual, or white-collar, workers are classified as middle class.[10] Alternatively, one may prefer to use income or education as measures of economic position, although these have some serious limitations. A given family income, for example, may imply many different economic circumstances, depending on such things as the geographical area or the age of the individual. A retired lawyer in a rural area might have a lower income than a factory worker in a big city, yet few people would claim that the factory worker was of higher social class or socioeconomic status. Use of education suffers from similar problems and also is confounded with age. Of course, occupation has its deficiencies as a measure of social class, but it probably is the best available indicator, and we shall relay on it in the following analysis.

Table 3.1 presents the voting behavior of working-class and middle-class individuals in presidential elections from 1952 to 1976. As a simple measure of the extent of class differences in voting, we may look at the difference between the Democratic percentages for the two classes.[11] This index of class voting, presented in Table 3.1, allows us to compare class voting in different elections. One point is immediately obvious: the degree of class voting fluctuates from one election to the next. The specific issues and candidates in each election accentuate or depress the degree of class voting, producing this variation over time.

Recent presidential elections illustrate why class voting fluctuates over time. In the 1972 election, which was marked by low class voting,

TABLE 3.1   Presidential Vote by Social Class, 1952–1976

	Year						
Social Class and Vote	1952	1956	1960	1964	1968	1972	1976
Working class:							
Democratic	57	52	60	82	58	38	63
Republican	43	48	40	18	42	62	37
	100	100	100	100	100	100	100
Middle class:							
Democratic	34	36	46	62	41	34	41
Republican	66	64	54	37	59	66	59
	100	100	100	100	100	100	100
Index of Class Voting	23	16	14	19	17	4	22

Figures represent the percentage presidential vote of working-class and middle-class individuals for each presidential election from 1952 to 1976. Nonvoters and those voting for minor party candidates (including Wallace in 1968) are excluded from this table. Social class was determined by the occupation of the head of the household, with blue-collar workers classified as working class and white-collar workers classifed as middle class. The index of class voting is the difference between the working-class Democratic percentage and the middle-class Democratic percentage. The larger the index, the greater the difference between the two social classes in their voting behavior.

Source: 1952–1960 data from Robert R. Alford, *Party and Society* (Chicago: Rand McNally, 1963), p. 352; 1964–1972 data from John W. Books and JoAnn B. Reynolds, "A Note on Class Voting in Great Britain and the United States," *Comparative Political Studies*, Vol. 18, No. 3 (October, 1975), p. 369; 1976 data from Bruce D. Bowen, C. Anthony Broh, and Charles L. Prysby, *Voting Behavior: The 1976 Election*, Supplementary Empirical Teaching Units in Political Science (Washington: American Political Science Association, 1978).

several noneconomic issues were important. These included: (a) the war in Vietnam and related problems, such as amnesty for draft evaders; (b) problems of crime, urban unrest, and violent protest, characterized as a general problem of law and order; and (c) conflict over the regulation of personal behavior and lifestyle, involving such moral issues as drug usage, pornography, and abortion. Many working-class voters held conservative attitudes on these issues and supported Nixon on that basis. McGovern's liberalism on these issues probably attracted liberal middle-class support while costing him votes among more conservative blue-collar groups. Also, unlike most Democratic presidential candidates, McGovern failed to receive the endorsement of many labor union leaders, including AFL-CIO head George Meany. In 1976 the issues and circumstances were different. Economic issues were more important (see Chapter 2) and the union movement was solidly behind Carter. As a result, Carter drew his support disproportionately from the working class.

It is worth noting that class voting has been weak or even nonexistent for several population groups. Among blacks, for example, middle-class voters are not more Republican than their working-class counterparts in their presidential voting.[12] White southerners also have been relatively undivided by class lines.[13] To the extent that class voting has been a feature of contemporary American politics, it has been located primarily among Northern whites, especially those in urban areas.

Presidential patterns may not be similar to those for other offices, so a more thorough comparison of class cleavages is presented in Table 3.2. In order to avoid confounding racial differences with class differences, the data are for whites only. Because blacks are both concentrated in the working class and overwhelmingly Democratic, looking at both racial groups together can give a misleading picture of the impact of class differences per se. The data in Table 3.2 show that class differences existed for congressional voting and party identification as well as for presidential voting in 1976. Since party identification is closely related to voting for most lower-level offices, this suggests that class cleavages are a feature of state and local elections as well as of national elections.

Only modest class differences in voting are evident in American elections. Although the working class is more Democratic in every election shown in Table 3.1, many middle-class voters cast Democratic ballots and many working-class individuals voted Republican. Moreover, class differences in voting behavior appear to be declining. Even considering the 1976 presidential election, it appears that class voting has been less pronounced in the 1970s than during the 1950s and 1960s.[14] Our pre-1950 data are less reliable, but the available evidence indicates that class voting was greater in the 1930s and 1940s than in

TABLE 3.2   Partisan Choice by Social Class for Whites, 1976

	Social Class	
	Working Class	Middle Class
Presidential Vote		
Carter	57	39
Ford	43	61
	100	100
(*N*)	(556)	(716)
Congressional Vote		
Democratic	60	47
Republican	40	53
	100	100
(*N*)	(457)	(581)
Party Identification		
Democratic	52	43
Independent	19	13
Republican	29	44
(*N*)	100	100
	(1054)	(1054)

Social class is defined by the occupation of the head of the household; blue-collar respondents are classified as working class and white-collar respondents are considered middle class. The data are for white respondents only. For party identification, the Democratic and Republican categories include the independent leaners; the independent category includes only the pure independents.

Source: Calculated from data provided by Bruce D. Bowen, C. Anthony Broh, and Charles L. Prysby, *Voting Behavior: The 1976 Election*, Supplementary Empirical Teaching Units in Political Science (Washington, D.C.: American Political Science Association, 1978).

the 1950s and 1960s.[15] Should this trend continue, the class basis of voting behavior may disappear or even be reversed, which would be a striking change in American politics. The potential significance of these developments leads us to consider why class voting has been declining.

One important development is the affluence of the post-World War II era. The median income among American families more than doubled between 1948 and 1972, even after correcting for inflation.[16] The increases in economic productivity and real income have produced a situation where the vast majority of Americans, according to some observers, can be considered middle class. Poverty still exists, to be sure, and most people still have economic concerns, but class differences in consumption patterns have been greatly reduced as the ownership of luxury goods has become more widespread.

Related to this increased affluence are changes in the occupational structure. The blue-collar labor force has become more skilled and better paid; unskilled laborers now constitute only 6 percent of the labor force.[17] The white-collar labor force has changed too, with a sizable expansion of nomanagerial employees. Many of these white-collar employees are in routine clerical, sales, and service positions that tend to be less skilled and more poorly paid. The result of these developments in the labor force is a blurring of the line between the manual and nonmanual strata, as many blue-collar workers find themselves as well off economically as many white-collar employees.

Young voters are especially unaffected by social class. Analyses of voting patterns of working-class and middle-class individuals in different age categories reveal that the difference between the two classes is greater for older voters.[18] The simplest explanation of the relationship between age and class voting lies in the experience of the different generations. Younger voters, lacking a direct experience with the Depression and having grown up in an age of affluence, do not respond to class-related appeals in the same way their elders do. To some extent, younger voters may be more influenced by class concerns as they age, but the evidence does suggest that true generational differences exist.[19]

In sum, an examination of data from the 1970s indicates that working-class individuals remain more likely than middle-class individuals to support Democratic candidates. However, contemporary class differences are modest in nature compared to those of earlier periods. Furthermore, class cleavages are weak or nonexistent for several important segments of the populations: blacks, southerners, and young people. The exact difference between social classes will vary, depending on the particular election we look at, but the long-run picture is one of limited polarization. This does not mean that economic position will fail to influence political attitudes or voting behavior. Occupational groupings will continue to have their own particular economic interests, and finer divisions may reveal interesting differences. For example, farmers, steel workers, truck drivers, policemen, and teachers will be concerned about different matters and will tend to differ on many issues. But the division between manual and nonmanual workers probably is becoming less relevant, for this line no longer neatly divides society into the haves and the have-nots.

Ethnic, Religious, and Racial Patterns

American political parties historically have reflected the sociocultural divisions in the society. The Democratic Party, at least since the 1930s, has been identified as the party of minority ethnic, religious, and racial groups. Part of this connection is due to to the relationship between social class and partisan choice, for sociocultural groups differ in their relative economic position, but more than merely class differences are involved. Historical ties, group identities and interests, and geographical factors all play a role.

Race stands out as the most important sociocultural factor in contemporary electoral politics. Two concurrent developments, both summarized in Table 3.3, have produced this situation. First, the black turnout rate has increased greatly, so that blacks are only marginally below whites in electoral participation. Second, blacks have become increasingly Democratic in their partisan tendencies, to the point that the black vote is almost homogeneous. The result of these changes is that blacks now constitute one of the important groups in the Democratic coalition. This was not the case in earlier years. Blacks were not a significant part of the original New Deal coalition, and even in the 1950s they did not contribute much to the Democratic vote. In the 1956 presidential election, for example, only 5 percent of Stevenson's votes came from the black population. But by the late 1960s this contribution had increased greatly; one out of every five voters for the Democratic presidential candidates in 1968 and 1972 was a black. In the tightly fought 1976 presidential election, Carter received one-sixth of his total vote from blacks, prompting many black leaders to claim that the black vote had given Carter the victory.[20]

The reasons for the developments shown in Table 3.3 are fairly obvious. The increased turnout represents an elimination of the legal barriers that prevented blacks from going to the polls (discussed in Chapter 2). The increased Democratic tendency is due to the behavior of the two parties. Blacks once supported the party of Lincoln, but as the

TABLE 3.3   Black Electoral Behavior, 1952–1976

Year	Percent Voting in the Presidential Election	Percent of Voters Voting for the Democrat Candidate
1952	23	83
1956	23	68
1960	31	72
1964	42	99
1968	51	92
1972	47	86
1976	49	95

Source: 1952–1972 data from Robert Axelrod, "Communications," *American Political Science Review*, Vol. 68, No. 2 (June, 1974), p. 718; 1976 data from Bruce D. Bowen, C. Anthony Broh, and Charles L. Prysby, *Voting Behavior: The 1976 Election*, Supplementary Empirical Teaching Units in Political Science (Washington: American Political Science Association, 1978). The 1976 turnout figure is an estimate arrived at by adjusting the survey data results to make them equal to the national turnout rate as estimated from aggregate census and election data.

Democratic Party became the champion of civil rights, the black vote moved in that direction. Democratic loyalty among blacks became extremely pronounced in the 1960s, as Lyndon Johnson's administration produced major civil rights legislation, and remained solidly Democratic in the 1970s. Of the major population groups, blacks are by far the most Democratic and most homogeneous in voting behavior.

Among whites, sociocultural divisions are more complex. The number of religious and ethnic divisions precludes a separate examination of each, but some general relationships can be discussed. These relationships should be understood as rough tendencies, for ethnic and religious groups rarely are cohesive and undifferentiated in their electoral behavior.

The basic generalization that can be made about ethnoreligious cleavages is that the more established groups are more Republican and the less established groups are more Democratic. By "more established groups" we refer to groups that immigrated relatively early, that were more easily assimilated in a social and cultural sense, and that have been more economically advantaged. The "less established groups" are those that arrived later, suffered more discrimination, and have been economically worse off. Among whites the Catholic–Protestant division is relevant. Many Catholics were first- and second-generation Americans whose ancestors were part of the wave of early twentieth century immigration that filled the blue-collar ranks of an industrializing America. These more newly arrived and less established groups have been disproportionately Democratic, as the data in Figure 3.1 illustrate. At the other end of the continuum, the upper-status Protestant groups—such as Episcopalians, Presbyterians, and Methodists—represent older immigrant groups from the British Isles, and they are the most Republican.[21]

Some complications may be pointed out. Among white Protestants, Baptists are the most Democratic. Yet Baptists are not a newly arrived or unassimilated group. The Democratic strength among Baptists is a result of their lower socioeconomic status and their geographical concentration in the South, which has been solidly Democratic for historical reasons. Jewish voters comprise another interesting group, for they have been quite Democratic despite relatively high socioeconomic status. Several factors may account for this apparent discrepancy: (a) Jews share several of the characteristics of other less-established groups, such as more recent time of arrival and lack of cultural assimilation; (b) liberal orientations are part of the Jewish religion and culture; and (c) Roosevelt's anti-Nazi foreign policy helped to bring Jews into the New Deal coalition.[22]

The last two factors mentioned above suggest two other general relationships. First, there may be some connection between religious

Figure 3.1
PRESIDENTIAL VOTING OF CATHOLICS AND PROTESTANTS,
1952–1976.

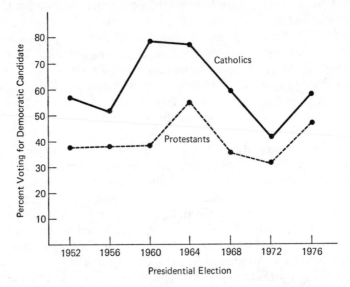

Source: 1952–1968 data from the *New York Times,* December 8, 1968, p. 84; 1972 and 1976 figures calculated from data provided by *Voting Behavior: The 1972 Election,* Supplementary Empirical Teaching Units in Political Science (Washington: American Political Science Association, 1975) and *Voting Behavior: The 1976 Election,* Supplementary Empirical Teaching Units in Political Science (Washington, D.C.: American Political Science Association, 1978), both by Bruce D. Bowen, C. Anthony Broh, and Charles L. Prysby.

doctrine and political orientation; religiously conservative churches (for example, the Mormans or the small fundamentalist Protestant sects) may have members who are politically conservative.[23] Second, specific issues and candidates influence the relationship between religion and partisan choice. The difference between Catholics and Protestants was accentuated in the 1960 presidential election because of Kennedy's Catholicism. Similarly, this Catholic–Protestant difference was somewhat lessened in the 1976 presidential contest, as a result of Catholic concerns over the fundamentalist Baptist background of the Democratic nominee. Also, the salience of and conflict over certain issues, such as publicly funded abortions, U.S. support for Israel, or regulation of pornography, may affect the religious basis of voting in specific elections.

Although the extent of religious differences in voting may vary from one election to the next, the long-run trend appears to be toward convergence of the Catholic and Protestant vote. This seems evident if we look at Figure 3.1; the difference between Catholics and Protestants in their presidential vote has declined in recent elections. This is in part a result of the continued assimilation of many of the formerly disadvantaged European ethnic groups. Ethnic identifications probably have weakened over time. As the old ethnic neighborhoods of Northern urban areas have broken apart, as individuals from different ethnic groups intermarry, and as ethnic groups become more economically diverse, ethnicity may be a less salient factor for many people.

Southern Voting Patterns

The most important regional division in American politics has been between the North and South. The distinctiveness of southern voting patterns.and the substantial change in these patterns have been important aspects of electoral politics over the past several decades. The old "solid South" was a region thoroughly dominated by the Democratic Party at all levels. The contemporary South, by contrast, is a region where Republicans have enjoyed at least modest electoral success, and not only in presidential elections. Republican governors, senators, and congressmen have been elected throughout the South.

The present level of Republican voting in the South appears more significant when put in historical perspective. From 1880 to 1944 the eleven states of the old Confederacy almost invariably supported the Democratic presidential nominee. Only in 1928 was the Republican candidate able to capture any substantial support in the South. Democratic strength in presidential elections was matched by domination of state and local elections. As late as 1948, only about 3 percent of all southern state legislators were Republicans, and five states had not a single Republican in either house of the state legislature.[24] The congressional elections of that year show an equally lopsided pattern: save for two Republican congressmen from Tennessee, every U.S. senator and representative from the South was a Democrat.[25]

Democratic hegemony was broken first in presidential elctions. The split at the 1948 Democratic convention, which led to the Dixiecrats capturing the electoral votes of four states in the deep South, signaled the start of a decline in the Democratic advantage in the South. Eisenhower carried several southern states in his victories, a remarkable achievement given the results of previous elections. Still, Eisenhower ran considerably worse in the South in terms of the popular vote, as his percentage in the South was six to seven points below his national percentage in both 1952 and 1956 (see Figure 3.2). This gap was narrowed by Nixon in 1960 to about two percentage points. In 1964 Goldwater became the first Republican presidential candidate in the twentieth century to actually run better in the South than in the North. Moreover, Goldwater captured the five states of the deep South, which made his base of support in the South different from that of Eisenhower and Nixon, who had much better success in the rim or border South. The disproportionate support that Goldwater received in the South was continued by Nixon in 1968 and 1972. In defeating McGovern, Nixon received 70 percent of the popular vote in the South, which was over 10 points more than his share of the vote outside the South.

This trend was reversed in 1976. Carter carried 10 of the 11 southern states, losing only Virginia to Ford. But looking at the electoral map and considering simply which way the states went tends to exaggerate Carter's success in the South. Despite his being a native southerner, Carter received only 54 percent of the popular vote in the South, which is not that much higher than the 51 percent he received nationally. This small difference is about equal to the advantage that Kennedy received in the South in 1960. Given the social and demographic characteristics of Carter and Kennedy, one would have suspected that Carter's appeal to the South would have been greater than Kennedy's. Furthermore,

Figure 3.2
PRESIDENTIAL VOTING IN THE SOUTH, 1952–1976.

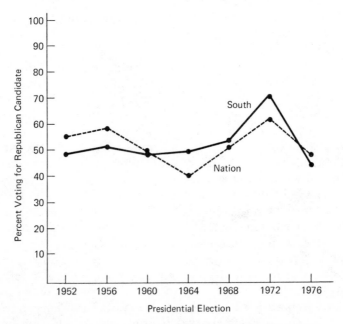

Source: Calculated from data in *Politics in America* (4th ed.; Washington D.C.: Congressional Quarterly, 1971), pp. 88–89; *Election '76* (Washington D.C.: Congressional Quarterly, 1976), pp. 104–105; and *Current American Government: Spring, 1977* (Washington D.C.: Congressional Quarterly, 1976), p. 3.

Carter obtained much of his vote in the South from blacks and received less than 50 percent of the southern white vote. In 1960 far fewer blacks voted in the South, so that Kennedy's support came primarily from the white southern electorate. This indicates how much change has occurred and how strong presidential Republicanism has become in the South.

Examining the results of presidential elections may give a misleading picture of Republican electoral strength in the South. Improvement below the presidential level has been much more limited and has occurred more slowly. The increase in presidential Republicanism during the 1950s was scarcely reflected at other levels. In 1960, for example, only 7 percent of the congressional seats and 4 percent of the state legislative seats were won by Republicans.[26] Substantial improvement did occur during the 1960s. By 1972, Republicans controlled approximately one-third of the U.S. Senate and House seats and over 15 percent of the state legislative seats in the region. But this long period of steady, if gradual, improvement was broken in 1974, and the Republicans were unable to recoup these losses in 1976. Currently, Republicans account for about 25 percent of the congressmen and about 10 percent of the state legislators in the South.[27] Although this is below the 1972 peak, it still is far greater than the comparable figures for the 1950s.

Republican voting is almost entirely limited to the white population, blacks being solidly Democratic, so we may focus on the factors that have influenced the electoral behavior of white southerners. Among whites, the important correlates of voting behavior have been socioeconomic status and geographical location, including both the urban–rural and the rim–deep South divisions. The distinction between the deep South and the rim South captures a number of social and historical differences. The five states of the deep South were the principal slave-holding states, and they currently are more rural and more black than the states of the rim South.[28]

The presidential Republicanism of the 1950s was located primarily in the rim South and in urban areas. Eisenhower and Nixon (in 1960) did their best in these areas. Furthermore, there was a middle-class bias to the Republican vote. In a sense, the New Deal class cleavages that existed in the North were being extended to the South. Middle-class voters were being attracted to the Republican Party on the basis of economic conservatism. Contributing to this tendency was the arrival of northern middle-class individuals, who settled principally in urban areas. These middle-class migrants were heavily Republican, reflecting the class polarization of the North, and they provided an important stimulus for the emerging Republicanism.[29]

A new source of Republican support developed during the 1960s. Goldwater did not draw votes primarily from the urban rim South, as

Eisenhower did; instead, his strong support came from the rural deep South, and he did much better among lower socioeconomic status voters than previous Republicans had.[30] The basis of the vote was different, too. Goldwater's appeal to southern whites was based on conservative civil rights orientations. Racially related issues had become more salient because of newly enacted and proposed civil rights legislation. George Wallace attracted much the same type of support in 1968, perhaps with other social and law and order issues adding to this appeal.

Both strains of potential support were tapped by Republican presidential candidates in the 1970s. Nixon and Ford attracted votes from whites in both urban and rural areas, in the deep South and the rim South, and among middle-class and working-class voters.[31] Republican voters were more conservative than Democratic voters on both economic issues and social-racial issues. As compared to Democratic voters, Republican voters are more antiunion, less supportive of social welfare measures, more opposed to civil rights measures and aid to minority groups, and generally conservative on questions of social control.[32] These different aspects of conservatism are related in different ways to geographical location and social status, so the result is that Republican presidential candidates have been able to draw support from almost all segments of the white population.

The South clearly is quite competitive when it comes to presidential elections. Below the presidential level, Republicans are weaker, but their position has improved. Democratic strength below the presidential level rests largely on better party organization and a greater number of office holders, both of which contribute to electoral success. Given the success that Republican presidential candidates have had in the region, even against a moderate southern Democrat, it is likely that Republican voting will increase at the lower levels, although perhaps in a slow and uneven manner.

THE CHANGING NATURE OF ELECTORAL POLITICS

The New Deal coalition still exists to some degree. Democrats continue to do better among southerners, working-class members and Catholics and other non-Protestant groups. But these tendencies are weaker than they once were. The differences in partisan preferences between the working and middle classes, between Catholics and Protestants, and between the South and the North have declined considerably over the past decades. These changes, moreover, do not appear to be temporary deviations, but rather part of long-run trends.

To understand more thoroughly the breakup of the New Deal coalition, we need to examine the attitudinal forces responsible for these changes. A review of some of the important issues that have been important in recent elections should allow for a better understanding of the changed nature of electoral politics.

The progressive weakening of the New Deal coalition is due largely to the changed issue agenda in American politics. The New Deal alignments were based primarily on economic orientations. The most important differences between the Democrats and Republicans were in their orientations on economic issues, with Democratic liberalism appealing more to the working class and lower socioeconomic status groups. But these economic issues have changed, new issues have become important, and the general liberal–conservative distinction has changed in meaning—all of which have been important.

Many of the fundamental economic issues of previous decades—coping with unemployment, regulating business and labor-management relations, providing social welfare benefits—remain important. But new economic issues have emerged in the 1970s as equally important, if not more so. Questions of handling inflation, energy shortages, and pollution and other environmental concerns are new and different issues. Liberal–conservative splits over these issues, if that ideological dimension can even be applied meaningfully here, may not be strongly related to the older liberal–conservative splits over economic issues. In particular, these issues do not divide along class lines in the way that other economic issues do, thus contributing to the declining class polarization in American politics.

Racial issues have become increasingly economic in nature. Prior to the mid-1960s, the important civil rights issues involved legal rights, such as the elimination of segregated facilities or ensuring the right to vote. Once the basic legal rights were established, attention was turned toward reducing the socioeconomic inequalities between blacks and whites. The question of how far the government ought to go in aiding blacks to improve their position has divided the old New Deal coalition. Many elements of the coalition, particularly ethnic working-class groups, are quite conservative on this issue. At the same time, blacks have become a very important part of the Democratic coalition. These conflicts are intense and unlikely to be resolved, so they probably will continue to be a source of tension within the Democratic Party.

Another source of conflict within the majority Democratic coalition is the increased salience of a set of social issues. These issues involve the appropriate government policies in the areas of criminal justice, personal behavior, and moral concerns. This diverse set of issues is loosely linked together; those with conservative orientations on these issues tend to stress the maintenance of social order and existing values and mores while those with liberal orientations favor less government regulation of personal behavior. Again, conservatism on these issues among parts of the New Deal coalition has been an important aspect of contemporary electoral politics.

The conservatism of several elements of the New Deal coalition on many comtemporary issues is quite apparent from any examination of recent public opinion data. But very liberal orientations on these issues are held by other components of the Democratic coalition, leading to intraparty conflict. These strains are greatest within the *national* Democratic Party. American political parties are sufficiently diverse and loosely structured to permit considerable regional variation. Thus, in some localities the Democrats may be predominantly liberal in orientation, while conservative attitudes may prevail in other areas. But at the national level these tensions are almost unavoidable, given the contemporary distribution of political attitudes. These tensions also exist within the Republican Party. Conflict between conservative and moderate Republicans was quite apparent in the 1976 presidential primaries, for example. But the Democratic Party, being larger and more diverse, seems more affected by the nature of contemporary issues.

The impact of new issues on the old party divisions has been, and probably will continue to be, heightened by the dealignment of the electorate. The declining partisanship, discussed in the previous chapter, means that more voters are splitting their ballots and switching between elections, making the party coalitions more unstable. Voters now are more responsive to short-term forces. The particular issues and candidates involved in the election are more important than before. All this makes for a more volatile electoral situation.

Candidates often find it difficult to deal with an intense and polarized set of opinions. They may find themselves besieged by single-interest groups, each having its own "acid test." The types of issues capable of generating such behavior are many and varied; recent examples include the Panama Canal treaties, nuclear power plant construction, legalized abortion, and busing for school integration. A candidate taking the "wrong" opinion on an issue of this sort may find that he cannot get the support of some group, regardless of his position on other issues. The natural tendency for a candidate in this situation may be to avoid taking definite stands on issues.

The changing nature of political issues and the changing nature of voter behavior may have an impact on how candidates run their campaigns and appeal for votes. Influence can occur in the other direction as well. Changing campaign methods may affect the way the electorate behaves. Voter behavior and candidate behavior are interrelated; we must examine both to understand the electoral process. Having discussed the behavior of voters, we turn to the behavior of candidates in the following chapters.

FOR FURTHER READING

James L. Sundquist, *Dynamics of the Party System,* [33] is an excellent discussion of the realignment process in general and the 1930s realignment in particular. Changes in the New Deal alignment are examined in *Transformations of the American Party System,* [34] by Everett Carll Ladd, Jr., with Charles D. Hadley. Class differences in electoral behavior are discussed in *Class and Politics in the United States,* [35] by Richard F. Hamilton. Religious and ethnic divisions are discussed by Albert J. Menendez, *Religion at the Polls,* [36] and Mark R. Levy and Michael S. Kramer, *The Ethnic Factor.* [37] Changes in southern politics are examined by Jack Bass and Walter DeVries, *The Transformation of Southern Politics.* [38]

NOTES

1. Walter Dean Burnham, *Critical Elections and the Mainsprings of American Politics* (New York: Norton, 1970), pp. 1–10.

2. James L. Sundquist, *Dynamics of the Party System* (Washington: The Brookings Institution, 1973), pp. 28–33.

3. V. O. Key, Jr., "Secular Realignment and the Party System," *Journal of Politics,* Vol. 21, No. 2 (May 1959), pp. 198–210.

4. Sundquist, *Dynamics of the Party System,* pp. 183–193.

5. Ibid., pp. 190-195.

6. Everett Carll Ladd, Jr., with Charles D. Hadley, *Transformations of the American Party System* (2nd edition; New York: Norton, 1978), p. 33.

7. Ibid., p. 51.

8. Ibid., p. 68.

9. Sundquist, *Dynamics of the Party System,* p. 209.

10.For people who are not heads of household, the usual procedure is to use the occupation of the household head. For retired people, the former occupation is used. Farmers are not usually classified in either class.

11. Robert R. Alford, *Party and Society* (Skokie, Ill: Rand McNally, 1963), pp. 79–86.

12. Ladd with Hadley, *Transformations,* p. 291.

13. Douglas S. Gatlin, "Party Identification, Status, and Race in the South: 1952-1972," *Public Opinion Quarterly,* Vol. 39, No. 1 (Spring 1975), pp. 39–51.

14. Ladd with Hadley, *Transformations*, pp. 284-290.

15. Alford, *Party and Society*, p. 227; Ladd with Hadley, *Transformations*, p. 101.

16. Ben J. Wattenberg, *The Real America* (New York: Putnam, 1976), p. 332.

17. Ibid., p. 324.

18. Paul R. Abramson, *Generational Change in American Politics* (Lexington, Mass.: Heath, 1975), pp. 30-36.

19. Ibid., pp. 37–41.

20. For 1956–1972 data see Robert Axelrod, "Communications," *American Political Science Review*, Vol. 68, No. 2 (June 1974), p. 718; the 1976 figure is estimated from survey data.

21. Albert J. Menendez, *Religion at the Polls* (Philadelphia: Westminster, 1977), pp. 123–132.

22. Ibid., pp. 113–117.

23. Ibid., pp. 169–173.

24. Jack Bass and Walter DeVries, *The Transformation of Southern Politics* (New York: Basic Books, 1976), pp. 34–37.

25. Ibid.

26. Ibid.

27. Ibid.

28. The deep South states are South Carolina, Georgia, Alabama, Mississippi, and Louisiana.

29. Paul Allen Beck, "Partisan Dealignment in the Postwar South," *American Political Science Review*, Vol. 71, No. 2 (June 1977), pp. 480–483.

30. Donald S. Strong, "Further Reflections on Southern Politics," *Journal of Politics*, Vol. 33, No. 2 (May 1971), pp. 239–256.

31. Charles L. Prysby, "Electoral Behavior in the American South: Recent and Emerging Trends," in *Party Politics in the South*, ed. by Robert Steed, Laurence Moreland, and Tod Baker (forthcoming).

32. Ibid.

33. Washington: The Brookings Institution, 1973.

34. New York: Norton, 1978 (2nd ed.).

35. New York: Wiley, 1972.

36. Philadelphia: Westminster, 1977.

37. New York: Simon & Schuster, 1972.

38. New York: Basic Books, 1976.

CHAPTER 4

The Campaign Begins

The American political system provides many potential avenues for citizens to influence their governments through the selection of political leaders. It also provides ample opportunity for those who want to run for public office. Hundreds of thousands of people avail themselves of this opportunity and enter the world of electoral politics. For the most part, they do so within the context of the two-party system, running either as a Democrat or as a Republican. Minor party candidates enter a number of elections but rarely win. The only significant exception to the pattern of two-party electoral politics is the existence in many cities and towns of nonpartisan local elections, in which candidates run only as individuals without any party labels appearing on the ballot. Political parties, then, affect and structure the recruitment of candidates for most elected offices, particularly the more significant ones. This does not mean, however, that candidates simply are selected by party oligarchs. The recruitment process is more complex than that, and it varies according to the type of office and the competitive status of the party organization in the area.

Why do people choose to run for public office? Once they decide to run, how do they attempt to secure their party's nomination and win election? These questions are taken up in this chapter. First, we shall look at the decision to run for office, examining the characteristics and circumstances that lead to becoming a candidate. Then we shall briefly outline the important aspects of campaigning and appealing to the electorate, topics to be discussed in more detail in Chapters 5–7. Finally, we discuss the general function of election campaigns as a part of the political process.

DECIDING TO BECOME A CANDIDATE

The reasons why people become candidates for public office are many and varied. The range of motives that people may have for running for office reflects the numerous types of offices that people can run for and the variety of political contexts in which people live and operate. Before outlining the motives that propel individuals into politics, let us look at three case studies. These cases do not exhaust the range of calculations that individuals considering a political campaign may make, of course, but they do illustrate some common reasons and considerations.

Case 1: Jimmy Carter's Presidential Bid The decision of Jimmy Carter (born James Earl Carter, Jr.) to seek the Democratic presidential nomination is interesting, in that Carter was not a well-known politician when he began his campaign. Prior to being elected president, Carter's political career had been brief. He was elected to the Georgia state senate in 1962, ran unsuccessfully for governor in 1966, and then was elected governor in 1970, serving from 1971 to 1975. Georgia law prohibited an incumbent governor from being reelected, so an individual with political ambition in that office had to aspire to another office.

Carter's attempt to capture the Democratic presidential nomination began while he was governor. At the 1972 Democratic National Convention, Carter indicated his interest in being the vice-presidential candidate.[1] This bid was not given serious consideration by the McGovern camp, but it does illustrate the ambitions that Carter held at that time. Following the convention, Carter began to think about running for president. Several friends and advisors suggested that he consider the possibility seriously. Hamilton Jordan, Carter's executive secretary, along with Jerry Rafshoon and others, argued that Carter should begin working for the presidential nomination.[2] Jordan prepared a lengthy memorandum in November 1972 describing a strategy for capturing the nomination.[3] Among the factors making a Carter bid feasible were the enhanced role of primaries in the nomination process and the advantage that a moderate Democrat might have after the McGovern defeat.

Carter's last two years as governor were spent laying the foundation for his presidential campaign. One important move was becoming chairman of the 1974 Democratic Campaign Committee. Although this was not a prestigious or sought-after position in most people's eyes, it provided Carter with access to key individuals within the Democratic Party, and the contacts that he made were utilized later in his campaign effort.

On December 12, 1974, as his term as governor was about to end, Carter formally announced his candidacy for the Democratic presidential nomination. Most observers considered him a very dark horse at that point, but Carter considered himself a serious candidate. He had been running for two years and was available for full-time campaigning in 1975 and 1976. His successful campaign for the nomination will be discussed in detail in Chapter 6.

Case 2: Texas Legislative Candidates, 1962   Looking at the decision of Carter to run for president provides us with an example of an elected official deciding to run for a higher office. We also want to know why people initially get involved in politics. To do this, we must look at a much lower level of office. The state legislature often attracts individuals running for the first time, and the position of state legislator is a common entry point into politics. For these reasons, we have selected a case study dealing with first-time candidates for state legislative office.

Let us look at candidates for the Texas state legislature from Travis County in 1962.[4] Travis County, which includes the capital city of Austin, had four seats in the Texas legislature in 1962, all elected on a county-wide basis. Fourteen candidates, mostly Democrats, sought election to these seats. Most of the candidates had never run for elected office previously. Two of these candidates may be looked at in some detail as examples of why individuals first decide to run for office.

One of the candidates sought the Democratic nomination for one of the seats. To be the Democratic nominee, he had to win a contested primary election. Victory in the primary election probably meant election to the office, given the strength of the Democratic Party in the area. The other candidate examined here sought the Republican nomination for another of the seats and was unopposed in the primary. But the ease of becoming the Republican candidate was matched by the difficulty of winning the general election while running under the Republican banner.

The Democratic candidate had a long-time interest in politics. Although he had never run for office himself, he had been active in campaigns and his father had been elected to state office. He had often thought of running before. The decision to run in 1962 was prompted by two considerations. First, the chances of beating the incumbent representative for the Democratic nomination looked particularly good that year. Several friends active in politics said that the incumbent was vulnerable. Also, personal factors were important in the calculation to run. The individual had changed jobs, had his own firm now, and had the time and freedom to run a campaign. Despite his deep interest in politics, he was unsure whether he would like being a legislator, but he did see a career in politics as a possibility.

Unlike the Democrat discussed above, the Republican was recruited by his party to be a candidate. He had considerable interest in politics and recently had become a Republican, but substantial persuasion was required to convince him to run, even though he was assured of the nomination. The heavy Democratic strength in the district discouraged potential Republican candidates, and the Republican county chairman saw candidacy as a party-building task as well as an effort at victory. The time demands of a campaign and the lack of available funds were factors discouraging candidacy. On the positive side, the particular legislative seat was seen as one that a Republican could win, as there was no incumbent and the Democratic Party was split. The Republican candidate felt that it was a good year for conservative candidates, which encouraged him to run. Also, although he had no prior political exposure, he did have some name recognition from his college athletic accomplishments.

Case 3: Rufus Edmisten, 1977 The cases we have described provide examples of the considerations that lead people to run for office. But not everyone who is interested in holding office actually runs for election. What sort of calculations lead individuals to not run for an office they would like to hold? One such case may provide some insight.

Jesse Helms, a conservative Republican, was elected to the U.S. Senate from North Carolina in 1972. Up for reelection in 1978, Helms was expected to face a difficult general election. The Democrats were the dominant party in the state; in fact, Helms was the only Republican elected as senator in North Carolina in the twentieth century. On the other hand, Helms had the advantages of incumbency, and he had considerable popularity among conservative Democrats.

In 1977, Democrats began to announce for the senatorial primary, scheduled for May 1978. Among the Democrats considering the race was Rufus Edmisten, the state attorney general and a former aide to retired Senator Sam Ervin. The general view was that if Edmisten decided to run, he would be a major contender for the Democratic nomination.[5] Having been elected attorney general twice, Edmisten had experience in statewide campaigning and more name recognition than most of the other Democratic candidates.

During the summer of 1977 Edmisten seriously considered running but avoided a formal declaration. He met with potential supporters and party leaders, and he employed pollster Peter Hart to conduct an opinion survey in North Carolina.[6] After reviewing the results of the survey and the other advice he received, Edmisten formally declared in November that he was not a candidate for the Senate. The perceived difficulty of beating Helms, along with the numerous contenders for the Democratic nomination, meant that Edmisten would have to be prepared for an expensive and time-consuming campaign.[7] Only in his mid-30s, Edmisten could afford to pass up this opportunity and wait for another, and hopefully better, one. As long as he remained attorney general, Edmisten would retain a strategic position for running for higher office.

Characteristics of Candidates

Running for office is an uncommon form of political participation. Only a small proportion, certainly less than 5 percent, of the adult population have ever run for public office.[8] Those who do usually have a high level of political awareness and past involvement. Even if we look at individuals who are running for office for the first time, we find that they generally have been interested in politics for a long time and have been active in various ways. Thus, candidates are not recruited evenly from the entire population, but disproportionately from the stratum of highly involved citizens.

Instances where a serious candidate for public office has not had a record of prior political activity generally involve cases where an individual has been motivated by some recent events or experiences. Someone who has had only modest political interest and involvement may become aroused by some political decisions or actions, perhaps because they affect him directly, and respond by filing for an elected public office. This usually occurs at the local level, concerning elections for such things as the city council, school board, or county commission.[9]

Becoming a candidate also depends on personal circumstances. For many candidates, one important factor is the support of family and friends. Running for public office exacts personal costs—time and money at least—and many individuals are reluctant to become a candidate without the support of relevant primary groups.[10] Often the individual's family and friends do more than just approve of a candidacy; they may play an important role in motivating the candidacy. There are many instances of individuals following other family members into politics. One of the legislative candidates discussed above had a parent who had been elected to state office, for example.

An equally important factor is the personal freedom to run. Many individuals lack the time and money to enter an election and serve in office. In most states, for example, the office of state legislator is a poorly paid, part-time position. Most state legislators find it necessary to maintain their occupation or business while serving in the legislature. But only a minority of people have occupations that permit this. A person in business for himself—a lawyer or insurance salesman, for example—may be able to combine public office with a private career. In fact, some people may find that holding public office furthers their private business or career. But for many people, occupational constraints preclude their holding many public offices. The case studies above illustrate the relevance of these personal factors. Both of the state legislative candidates were in business situations that provided sufficient freedom to run. Similarly, the ability of Jimmy Carter to campaign full-time for over one year before the first presidential primary (while his brother minded the family peanut business) undoubtedly influenced his decision to run.

The occupation most associated with American politics is that of lawyer. Woodrow Wilson stated simply, "The profession I chose was politics; the profession I entered was the law. I entered one because I thought it would lead to the other."[11] Several reasons are behind the overrepresentation of lawyers in politics:

> The lawyer may be able to crowd his gainful labors into the legislative schedule. . . . He possesses the verbal skills we associate with the legislative life, and his very training in the law singularly equips him, in eyes of most voters, to make law. . . . These occupations . . . are the ones that will profit from the contacts the legislator makes. . . . It is almost the classic career pattern for the new young lawyer in town to build his practice in part through the pursuit of public office. . . . To sum up, the legislator's occupation must offer a number of assets: free time, public contacts, favorable vocational training, and social status. The occupation of the lawyer in American society offers them all par excellence.[12]

In general, candidates are not representative of the general population in social or demographic terms. They are higher in social status, usually having a college degree and a professional or managerial occupational background. Also, most candidates are white males, although the number of women and blacks running for public office has been increasing. Candidates tend to have these social characteristics in part because there traits are associated with political involvement and personal opportunity and in part because people with these characteristics find it easier to obtain support for their candidacy.

Political Opportunity and Candidate Recruitment

Becoming a candidate depends upon having an appropriate political opportunity. Individuals are more likely to run for office if they perceive some chance of winning. The required magnitude of that perceived chance varies enormously from one person to the next. In the case studies discussed above, Edmisten was reluctant to run for the Senate unless his perceived chance of success was quite high, while Carter was willing to run for president with a much lower probability of success. Of course, Carter was unable to remain governor, so he had to run for some other office if he wanted to continue his political career, whereas Edmisten could probably remain attorney general for some time. This leads to the generalization that the opportunity to run for a specific office is evaluated in terms of the individual's current situation. A governor who cannot run again may be quite willing to chance an attempt at a Senate seat that will be difficult to win, while a congress-man who can almost certainly be reelected may be unwilling to give up his seat and take such a gamble, for example.

Individuals sometimes become candidates even when the perceived chance of being elected is extremely low. There are several reasons why this occurs. The experience of running may make the difference in a subsequent try for office. Individuals sometimes run for office to help out their party, which may be having difficulty recruiting candidates for some places on the ballot. We also find individuals running for office without any interest in being elected, such as the various minor party candidates who run and get only a miniscule fraction of the vote. Their candidacy reflects a desire to have a vehicle for expressing their politi-cal views, not a desire to win office. Similar candidates appear in the primary elections of the major parties, along with other candidates who seem to want only the publicity obtained from the campaign. The various frivolous candidates found at all levels may be interesting, but our concern is with candidates who have a more serious interest in being elected.

In some cases the idea of running for public office originates with the candidate himself. In other instances, the original impetus comes from external factors, particularly parties and interest groups. Both self-start-ers—those who initiate their own candidacy—and reluctants—those recruited by others—frequently are found running for office. For exam-ple, one study of recruitment patterns to state legislative office found about half of the legislative candidates to be self-starters and half to be reluctants.[13]

Political parties are especially likely to actively recruit candidates when there is a lack of qualified individuals anxious to run under the party label. This has a great deal to do with the competitive status of the party. A minority party in an area may have to work hard to recruit candidates for what almost certainly will be losing efforts. The majority party in the same area will have far less difficulty putting people on the ballot. The availability of qualified candidates depends on the office as well as the status of the party. Even a minority party facing a popular incumbent president will have no lack of individuals willing to run under the party label. For less prestigious offices, far fewer candidates will be anxious to run.

Political Ambition and Political Careers

Among those who want to hold political office, the extent of political ambition varies enormously.[14] Some desire only to be elected to a single office for a single term. The Texas legislative candidates discussed above exhibited these feelings; both claimed that, if elected, they were not sure that they wanted to serve more than one term. Wanting no more than a single term in a single office is particularly common at the lower levels of elected office.

Some individuals wish to capture a specific office and hold it for a number of terms. The congressman and senator who make careers of being in Congress exemplify this possibility. Finally, some individuals desire to move up the political ladder through election to several offices. Carter is a good example of a person who had such ambitions and who was able to fulfill them.

Ambition often changes over time. The legislative candidate with limited ambition may find after he is elected that he would like a career in elected politics; the senator who has desired only a career in the Senate may come to decide that he would like to be president; and the individual with ambitious career plans may decide, after attaining the position of governor, that he has lost interest in seeking further elected office.

Political ambition leads people to run for office and, in some cases, to attempt a political career. Political careers in American politics exhibit structure and regularity, particularly for those who are elected to the higher level offices. The patterns that political careers assume are tendencies, not absolutes. There are no legal requirements that individuals have to start their political careers at certain points or progress in certain ways, and so there are many exceptions to the general patterns described below.

Common entry points in politics can be identified. Individuals generally do not run for a high-level office without prior office-holding experience. Frequent points of entry are the state legislature, local elected office, and the various law enforcement offices.[15] Different patterns exist in different states, depending in part on the supply of elected offices of each type. Judges, for example, are elected in some states and appointed in others. In general, election to the state legislature is the most common prior experience of those who run for higher office, such as governor, senator, or congressman. Jimmy Carter's first elected office was state senator, for example.

Following their entry into politics, those who move up to higher office tend to progress along established patterns. Candidates for U.S. senator often hold the office of governor or U.S. representative. Congressional candidates frequently have been previously elected to the state legislature or to one of the various law-enforcement offices, such as district attorney or a minor judgeship. Certain offices are common stepping stones to other offices. The office of state attorney general, for example, often is filled by individuals who attempt to move up to higher elected office.[16]

Several reasons can be given for these patterns of office holding. One important factor is the congruence of electorates.[17] For example, a governor and a senator in a state both share the same electorate. A governor may feel that since he has won a statewide election to become governor, he could win a statewide election for the U.S. Senate. Also, some offices are similar in function.[18] For example, a state legislator may feel he is a logical candidate for the Congress, or a congressman may think he is a logical choice for the Senate, because such a move would be from one legislative position to another.

Interesting changes in presidential recruitment patterns have occurred over the past two decades. John F. Kennedy in 1960 was the first U.S. senator nominated for president by the Democratic Party since 1860. During that century, governors were most frequently nominated by both parties. The importance of convention bargaining on the outcome of nomination battles during this period put large-state governors, able to deliver their state's delegate votes, in an advantageous position. The introduction and spread of state presidential primaries, along with altered convention rules, changed these patterns. The mass media and the general electorate became more directly involved in the nomination process. The increasing role of the national government in American life, and the increasing importance of foreign relations, focused the attention of the news media on Washington, and in particular on the White House and the Senate. As national television networks developed, and located their political correspondents in Washington, it became more difficult for governors to match the media coverage accorded to senators.

Between 1960 and 1976, 16 of the 21 presidential and vice-presidential nominees had served in the Senate. Only 2 of the 21 candidates (Jimmy Carter and Spiro Agnew, vice president under Nixon) had served as governor, and neither got on the national ticket because of his ability to swing home-state convention votes. Thus, senators, not governors, have become the prime source of presidential candidates. The vice-presidency, an office often filled by a former senator, also stands out as an important stepping stone to the presidency. Four recent presidential nominees (Nixon, Johnson, Humphrey, and Ford) had served as vice-president.

The nominations of 1976 were different from other recent experiences. Carter defeated several U.S. senators for the Democratic nomination and became the first former governor elected president since Franklin Roosevelt. Similarly, another former governor, Ronald Reagan, almost defeated President Ford for the Republican nomination. If the events of 1976 suggest that senators will not always dominate presidential nomination contests, they do not speak to the advantage senators, free of executive responsibilities, have over governors in finding time to campaign in primaries across the country. Neither Carter nor

Reagan were incumbents. Senators and vice presidents will be likely to continue to enjoy an advantage over others in the search for media attention, funds, and leadership support. The relative electoral security and longer terms of office that senators have give them greater opportunities to build support outside their home states. On the other hand, the 1976 campaign demonstrated the attractiveness to many voters of the "outsider" image put forward by Carter and Reagan, an image that probably will be exploited again by candidates unassociated with Washington and the presumed mistakes of the past.

THE ESSENTIALS OF A CAMPAIGN

Most candidates for public office must put together an effective campaign organization, often for both a primary and a general election. Some candidates are fortunate enough to avoid this. In any given congressional election year, for example, there will be a number of representatives who will be reelected without facing any significant competition. Election to local office sometimes requires no campaigning, particularly for an incumbent seeking reelection. But for most offices, and particularly the more significant ones, candidates must run an effective campaign, which involves both acquiring sufficient resources and using the resources in an effective manner. The campaign components outlined below will be elaborated upon in Chapter 5.

Campaign Financing

Money is a most important resource for campaigns. It is extremely convertible and transferable, as it can be converted into a number of useful things for a campaign and transferred from one area to another as campaign needs dictate. Money is, as one politician put it, "the mother's milk of politics."[19]

Campaign expenditures go for a variety of things. The purchase of television and radio time can use up a substantial portion of campaign resources. Broadcast expenditures at all election levels totaled about $60 million in 1972, or about one-seventh of all campaign spending.[20] Besides broadcast expenditures, advertising through newspapers and mass mailings takes a significant share of campaign funds. Money also goes for a variety of campaign services. Professional pollsters, advertising agencies, campaign managers, and fund-raising consultants are regularly employed by candidates for higher-level offices. Finally, money must be available for establishing campaign headquarters, providing for sufficient travel, and purchasing campaign materials.

Campaigns have become increasingly expensive. Increases are especially visible at the presidential level. In 1960, Richard Nixon and John Kennedy each spent about $10 million.[21] In 1972, Nixon spent six times that amount to get reelected. George McGovern spent $30 million in his losing campaign, more than any previous presidential candidate had spent.[22] Public financing is now available for presidential candidates. In 1976, the two major candidates each were entitled to $21.8 million for their general election campaign.[23]

Looking at presidential election expenditures can give a misleading picture of campaign financing in general. Of the elected offices in this country 95 percent probably require less than $10,000 to wage a competitive campaign, and many take no more than $1,000.[24] For these offices the candidate can usually rely on his own funds, contributions from friends and associates, and money obtained from informal fund-raising efforts.

The offices that usually require substantial campaign funds are, besides the presidency, the other elected national offices and the more visible state-wide offices. Gubernatorial election expenses naturally vary with the state. A large and competitive state can require a million-dollar campaign. Ronald Reagan spent $5 million getting elected governor of California in 1966, and Nelson Rockefeller spent $8 million in his 1970 reelection as governor of New York.[25] U.S. senatorial candidates in large states often spend over a million dollars. A candidate in a safe rural congressional district might spend only a few thousand dollars, but a competitive urban House seat will require $100,000 or more in campaign funds. Even lesser offices can be expensive in some cases. Running for the California State Senate from a competitive district was estimated to cost $20,000, and becoming county executive in populous Suffolk county, Long Island, will require $100,000.[26]

Spending a great deal of money does not guarantee victory, but candidates nevertheless feel compelled to spend. If nothing else, spending tends to keep the campaign active and the workers enthusiastic. Although there is usually no clear idea of the number of additional votes that will be produced by a given increase in campaign spending, there is the assumption that somehow the spending will do some good. As one observer put it, "perhaps half of all campaign spending is wasted—but no one knows which half."[27]

Campaign Personnel

The size and nature of the campaign staff depends on the extent of the campaign desired by the candidate and on the resources available. The higher and more visible offices generally require larger and more skilled campaign staffs, and this often means use of professionals. A candidate for local office is likely to make do with a few friends and relatives who volunteer to help in the campaign. On the other hand, a candidate for governor or U.S. senator probably will have a large staff, with heavy reliance on professional consultants and campaign firms. In the more populous states, a senatorial or gubernatorial campaign might easily have over 100 people, paid and unpaid, significantly involved.

Candidates can recruit their campaign staffs from three sources: the relevant party organization, professional campaign specialists, and volunteers. Traditionally, nominees turned to their political party for assistance. In some cases, the party organization still essentially runs the campaign. In other cases, the candidate receives virtually no assistance from the party organization in his area. Most candidates find themselves between these two extremes. Many candidates must develop their own campaign organization simply because the local party organization is too weak. Even where the candidate can rely on his party organization for significant help in the general election, he is likely to be on his own in the primary election and thus will be forced to develop his own personal organization.

The tendency of candidates to rely on professional help rather than the party organization is reflected in the growth of campaign management firms since the first was formed in California in 1934.[28] Growth of this industry was extremely limited until the 1950s. Rapid growth did not come about until the 1960s, however. No more than 25 congressional candidates had a professionally managed campaign in 1960, for example, but by 1968, about 125 candidates for the House used a professional campaign management firm.[29] This trend has accelerated in the 1970s.

Professional campaign firms supply a wide range of services. Some provide complete campaign management. These firms will take over the entire responsibility of running the campaign, from planning campaign strategies to supervising the day-to-day operations. Others provide more specialized services. Candidates intending to make extensive use of the media are likely to employ a professional advertising agency or media consultant to supervise the media campaign. Professional pollsters are increasingly being employed by candidates. A number of other consultants may be employed, including speech writers, legal consultants, computer programmers, and statisticians.

Most of the people who work in a campaign are not paid professionals. Volunteer workers are important for such things as canvassing neighborhoods, telephoning potential supporters, and distributing campaign materials. Recruiting a sufficient number of volunteers may not be an easy task for a candidate, however, as only a small proportion of the population participates in election campaigns. A survey of the American adult population in 1967 found that only about one-fourth had ever worked in an election campaign.[30] The number involved in any one year is far less than that, and the number working in any given election campaign even smaller. Probably no more than 5 percent of the adult population worked in the campaigns of the various presidential contenders in 1976.[31]

Campaigns and the Political Process

Election campaigns are a significant part of the American political process. One sign of their importance is the amount of media coverage that election campaigns, particularly national ones, attract. Another sign of this importance is the number of electoral reforms that have been recently enacted or proposed, such as those dealing with campaign finance. The exact role or function of election campaigns, as a part of the political process, may not be clear, however. Put simply, what is it that campaigns are supposed to do? The general answer to this question is that campaigns should help the voters acquire information about the candidates, thereby leading to a more informed vote. One way to assess campaigns, then, is in terms of the quality of this information flow.

Campaigns should provide an opportunity for voters to learn about the issue positions of the candidates. We think it desirable for voters to be aware of what the candidates stand for and to cast their ballots accordingly, and campaigns ideally should further this awareness and behavior. Looking at it from another perspective, campaigns should provide an opportunity for candidates to put forth policy proposals and attempt to convince voters of the desirability of these policy stands.

In reality, election campaigns may not be so educational. Candidates may fail to take clear policy stands. Campaign statements frequently consist of vague statements that identify problems and state desired goals. For example, a candidate may charge that the high cost of living is a problem and that the government needs to take action to hold down inflation. But unless these vague statements are backed up by more specific proposals, the candidate's statements are not informing the voters very much at all. Even when candidates do take specific positions, they may be careful to see that only a select audience receives the message. In speaking before a particular group a candidate may endorse specific proposals that the group desires, but statements on the same topic intended for a wider audience may be more vague. In short, candidates often find it desirable or advantageous to be ambiguous about their policy stands.[32]

Campaigns also allow the voters to assess the personal characteristics of the candidates. As we have seen earlier, perceptions of the personal qualities of the candidates play an important role in voting behavior. Voters are not likely to cast their ballots for candidates that they perceive as lacking in leadership ability, trustworthiness, or good judgment, even if they agree with the policy stands of the candidates. How the candidates react to the events, pressures, and crises of the campaign affects how the voters assess the abilities of the candidates. Recent presidential elections provide examples of this. In 1972, George McGovern was hurt by his handling of the crisis that occurred when it was revealed that his first vice-presidential nominee, Tom Eagleton, had received electric shock treatments for mental depression. Jimmy Carter's image also suffered some damage following the appearance in *Playboy* magazine of an interview with him in which he made some embarrassing remarks.

How accurately voters can assess the personal qualifications of the candidates is a key question. Some analysts argue that candidates are all too able to manipulate their public image through careful and controlled presentation of themselves in the media. Others claim that unimportant incidents or statements can be blown out of proportion by the national news media. During the second 1976 presidential debate, Ford made a comment about Poland not being under the domination of the Soviet Union. That single statement attracted considerable media attention over the next few days and proved to be a great embarrassment. Similar examples can be found in other elections. George Romney's chances of obtaining the 1968 Republican presidential nomination supposedly were severely damaged by his statement that he had been "brainwashed" by the American military when he visited Vietnam. But whether one or two statements provide a reliable guide to candidate's personal qualifications and capabilities certainly seems questionable. Perhaps many voters do not obtain from the campaign the type of information that is needed to form an accurate judgment about the personal qualities of the candidates.

Election campaigns may or may not fulfill the role that we think they should have in the American political process. Much depends on how the campaigns are conducted. The following chapters take up this topic in more detail, examining how candidates appeal for votes. A more thorough knowledge of campaign methods and practices will allow us to better assess the value of elections and campaigns as a part of the political system.

FOR FURTHER READING

The recruitment of candidates for lower-level offices is discussed by James David Barber, *The Lawmakers,* [33] Kenneth Prewitt, *The Recruitment of Political Leaders: A Study of Citizen-Politicians,* [34] and Lester G. Seligman et al., *Patterns of Recruitment.* [35] Joseph A. Schlesinger, *Ambition and Politics,* [36] contains information on political careers. The development of modern campaign methods is described in David Lee Rosenbloom, *The Election Man,*[37] and Dan Nimmo, *The Political Persuaders.*[38] An assessment of campaigning at the presidential level is provided by Stephen Hess, *The Presidential Campaign.*[39]

NOTES

1. Martin Schram, *Running for President* (New York: Pocket Books, 1976), pp. 61–63.

2. Jules Witcover, *Marathon* (New York: Viking, 1977), pp. 108–110.

3. Ibid., pp. 110–115.

4. The information on these candidates was provided by David M. Olson, who interviewed the participants in that election. Because the interviews were conducted under a promise of confidentiality, the names of the candidates are not given.

5. *Greensboro Daily News,* June 12, 1977, p. 1

6. *Raleigh News and Observer,* August 8, 1977, p. 8

7. *Charlotte Observer,* November 17, 1977, p. 1

8. Lester W. Milbrath and M. L. Goel, *Political Participation* (2nd ed; Skokie, Ill.: Rand McNally, 1977), pp. 18–19.

9. Kenneth Prewitt, *The Recruitment of Political Leaders: A Study of Citizen-Politicians* (Indianapolis: Bobbs-Merrill, 1970), p. 60.

10. Lester G. Seligman et al., *Patterns of Recruitment* (Skokie, Ill.: Rand McNally, 1974), pp. 182–184.

11. Quoted in Joseph A. Schlesinger, *Ambition and Politics* (Skokie, Ill.: Rand McNally, 1966), p. 17.

12. Frank J. Sorauf, *Party and Representation* (New York: Atherton, 1963), p. 73.

13. Seligman, *Patterns of Recruitment,* p. 72.

14. See Schlesinger, *Ambition and Politics,* for a more thorough discussion of political ambition.

15. Ibid., pp. 70–88, 91–95.

16. Ibid., pp. 61–67.

17. Ibid., pp. 99.

18. Ibid., pp. 99–100.

19. George Thayer, *Who Shakes the Money Tree?* (New York: Simon & Schuster, 1973), p. 208.

20. Herbert E. Alexander, *Financing Politics* (Washington: Congressional Quarterly, 1976), p. 27.

21. Ibid., p. 20.

22. Ibid.

23. *Elections '76* (Washington: Congressional Quarterly, 1976), p. 70.

24. Thayer, *Who Shakes the Money Tree?* p. 165.

25. Ibid., p. 166.

26. Ibid.

27. Alexander, *Financing Politics,* p. 57.

28. David Lee Rosenbloom, *The Election Men* (New York: Quadrangle Books, 1973), pp. 45–46.

29. Ibid., p. 11.

30. Sidney Verba and Norman H. Nie, Participation in America (New York: Harper, 1972), p. 351.

31. Center for Political Studies, *The CPS 1976 American National Election Study,* Vol. 1 (Ann Arbor, Michigan: Inter-University Consortium for Political and Social Research, 1977), p. 262.

32. Benjamin I. Page, *Choices and Echoes in Presidential Elections* (Chicago: University of Chicago, 1978), pp. 152–179.

33. New Haven, Conn.: Yale University Press, 1965.

34. Indianapolis: Bobbs-Merrill, 1970.

35. Skokie, Ill.: Rand McNally, 1974.

36. Skokie, Ill.: Rand McNally, 1966.

37. New York: Quadrangle Books, 1973.

38. Englewood Cliffs, N.J.: Prentice-Hall, 1970.

39. Washington: The Brookings Institution, 1974.

CHAPTER 5

The Campaign Organization

Over a four-year period more than 500,000 public offices are filled by election in the United States—more per capita than in any other country in the world. Unlike most other democracies, the United States is characterized by long and expensive campaigns and, unlike those in most other democracies, party organizations in the United States tend to be scrawny creatures unequipped for such arduous efforts. What has arisen to play the leading role in campaigns is the candidate-centered organization, an organization brought into existence to advance a particular candidate in a particular race.

In this chapter we will discuss major trends in political campaign organization and methods, and examine their implications for candidates and for the electoral system. Increasingly, during the past three decades, candidates for political office (a) *have been able to learn more about voters and what they want;* (b) *have been able to reach more voters with less mediation by others;* and (c) *have been able, or have been forced, to campaign for longer periods, with more money and more professional staffs.* Associated with the first trend have been new research methods (opinion polling). Associated with the second trend have been new media of communication (television, computerized direct mail) and the weakening of political parties. Associated with the third trend have been changes in nomination politics (for example, more Presidential primaries), new financing opportunities (public financing), and the availability of new campaign professionals. Affecting all of these trends are new financing restraints imposed by federal and state governments.

These trends suggest that every candidate must deal with several basic problems relating to campaign organization and methods. As is true of decision-makers in any organization, the candidate must make initial choices as to how inevitably limited resources will be utilized, and how future choices are to be made. *The candidate must raise and spend money. The candidate must learn about the electorate. The candidate must reach voters.* Around these major problems this chapter will be organized.

CANDIDATE CHOICES

At the outset of a campaign the candidate and campaign managers usually agree on a plan. Usually, the higher the office, the more elaborate and detailed is the plan. For lower offices the plan may be simply a list of things to do written on the back of an envelope. Often the plan is adopted and other campaign-management decisions are made by borrowing from experience, one's own and others', whatever seems to be relevant. Candidates and managers apparently develop plans by following approaches learned in previous campaigns, through personal experience of other kinds, and by imitating the behavior of other similarly situated candidates.[1]

Most plans sequence campaign events by time. Campaign managers know by tradition, if not from data, when people are inclined to contribute money or work for a candidate. Survey data suggest when voters are likely to begin paying attention to a candidate, and when vote choices are likely to be made by different groups in the electorate. Changes in finances or other resources, of course, can considerably alter the interrelationships between stages and components in a campaign plan. For a local campaign the plan, or activity calendar, might cover only the six months before the first vote. For a statewide campaign a plan usually is agreed upon a year before the primary election. Gubernatorial candidates and, more frequently, presidential candidates begin their efforts as soon as the previous election is over—almost four years ahead of time.

The recruitment or self-recruitment of candidates was discussed in Chapter 4. Once the decision to run has been made (but before a formal announcement of candidacy), it is to the candidate's friends and neighbors that he or she must look for early money and initial contacts. The first financial contributors are asked to contact *their* friends and neighbors, and thus begins the card file of contributors upon which the campaign must rely. The candidate and his or her friends contact newspaper editors, party officials, and interest group leaders. The box, "The Jordan Memo," suggests the early concern with press relations in the

The Jordan Memo

Hamilton Jordan, an aide to then Governor Jimmy Carter, wrote a memorandum on November 4, 1972, the day before Richard Nixon's landslide re-election. The memo outlined what Carter needed to do to win the Democratic presidential nomination in 1976. Among other things, Jordan suggested:

> ... It is necessary that we begin immediately to generate favorable stories and comments in the national press. Stories in the *New York Times* and *Washington Post* do not just happen, but have to be carefully planned and planted. ... The thrust of your national press effort should be that state government is working in Georgia. ... By emphasizing this theme and making your own political plans a secondary consideration, I believe you would have the forum and excuse you need to appear on television talk shows, write articles for national publications. ... Develop and/or maintain a close personal relationship with the principal national columnists and reporters. ... Fortunately, a disproportionate number of these opinion-makers are southerners by birth and tradition. ...*

*Martin Schram, *Running for President* (New York: Pocket Books, 1976), pp. 67–69.

1976 Carter presidential campaign. As the candidate consults (often, in fact, simply informs) leaders of the party of his or her intentions, these leaders are given an opportunity to "place their bets" on the candidate, or at least to observe and appraise the candidate in person.

The core personnel for the campaign organization must be identified; a campaign manager is chosen, or emerges. Political acquaintances, friends, staff members of the candidate, or professionals are put in charge of the financial, mass media, legal, volunteer, and research aspects of the campaign. Or, in a local campaign, one person may handle all of these tasks.

Money and people are the essential ingredients in a campaign. To some extent an abundance of one can make up for the lack of the other. A rich campaign organization can hire professionals to do the work for which there are no volunteers. An organization with little money can rely on the labor of supporting groups and individuals. In a local campaign there will rarely be funds to hire more than one professional, if that, and in a presidential campaign professionals will be involved in almost every facet of the campaign. At the statewide or congressional level, there is more variability in the extent to which a candidate calls upon campaign professionals. The types of expertise available are varied: direct mail for fund-raising and canvassing purposes; opinion polls; media buying and program production; legal and accounting assistance. All of these tasks require money, but even if the candidate chooses not to rely on professionals, all campaigns must be financed. So we will turn now to a discussion of campaign financing.

FUND-RAISING

Efforts to control campaign finance have been justified by the belief that some parties and candidates are disadvantaged by unfettered fund-raising, and thus the public's opportunity to choose freely is limited. However, all restrictions work to the disadvantage of some more than others, and given that the mind of man is constantly devising ways to circumvent inconvenient restrictions, it is not surprising that enforcement of campaign-financing restrictions has proved to be difficult.

Legislation in 1867 and 1883 was designed to protect federal employees from being required to contribute funds for political purposes —a common occurrence in the nineteenth century, and common enough at the state and local level into the twentieth century. Four federal laws, enacted between 1907 and 1925, required disclosure of campaign contributions and banned contributions by corporations. But these laws were not enforced. The electoral reform legislation of the 1970s involved more far-reaching changes than any previous period.

Changing the Rules

In the two decades between the year of Dwight Eisenhower's first election (1952) and the year of Richard Nixon's reelection (1972), the cost of all political campaigns rose from $140 million to $425 million. The Nixon campaign in 1972, the year of the Watergate affair, spent an unprecedented $61 million on the way to winning an overwhelming vote. Money always has played a controversial part in American politics, but it was the 1972–1974 Watergate affair (see the "Watergate" box) that proved to be the central event in a remarkable period of campaign finance reform. Many people came to feel that one of the lessons of Watergate was that too much money was too easily available from too many suspect sources with too little scrutiny of the uses to which it was put, and that something should be done about this.

Changes made or proposed in campaign financing in the 1970s included these:

In 1970 a fairly narrow campaign finance reform bill passed Congress but was vetoed by President Nixon.

Watergate

Republican Richard Nixon, elected President in 1968, was campaigning for reelection in 1972. On the night of June 17, 1972, a night watchman at the Watergate office building noticed a door taped open and called the police. Five men were arrested in the offices of the chairman of the Democratic National Committee. The next two years witnessed a series of revelations about the campaign practices and other activities of the Nixon Administration—revelations that led ultimately to the resignation of President Nixon. His campaign organization had authorized the Watergate break-in and other illegal activities, and once the Watergate burglars were arrested the White House engaged in an elaborate effort to cover up its ties to Watergate. These efforts involved significant amounts of money raised as campaign funds. Contributions tend to flow to incumbents who are expected to be reelected. Thus, in the months prior to April 7, 1972 (the date the new Federal Election Campaign Act was due to take effect, and after which campaign contributions would have to be made public), Nixon fund-raisers Maurice Stans and Herbert Kalmbach moved through the boardrooms of American business gathering the millions that were to be spent. Later more than 20 corporations, including several of the largest in the country, pleaded guilty to making illegal corporate contributions in 1972.

Obstruction of justice, perjury, and other charges led to the conviction and imprisonment of more than a dozen high Nixon Administration officials. President Nixon himself was on the verge of being impeached by the U. S. House of Representatives when he resigned. Shortly afterward, before any criminal charges could be brought against Nixon, President Ford gave him a pardon for any crimes associated with Watergate.

In 1971 Common Cause, a national "citizen's lobby," sued the Republican and Democratic Parties for violating the Federal Corrupt Practices Act of 1925. This act, among other things, had set a ceiling of $5,000 on political contributions from any individual. This ceiling had been ignored with impunity for many years by contributors to both parties.

The Federal Election Campaign Act of 1971, which took effect the next April, and the Revenue Act of 1971 introduced major changes in the intake, outgo, and reporting of campaign funds. Both were to be substantially revised by amendments in 1974. Thus, these laws took effect in the midst of a presidential campaign, and were revised by the time of the next presidential campaign.

Between 1974 and 1976 49 states revised their laws on campaign finance. An example was passage of California's Proposition 9 in 1974.[2]

The Federal Election Campaign Act Amendments of 1974 imposed a variety of restrictions, discussed in the next section. The Federal Election Commission (FEC) mandated by the 1974 act did not become operational until spring 1975, however, and shortly afterward it was idled by a court challenge.

In January 1976 the U.S. Supreme Court in *Buckley vs. Valeo,* upheld the major provisions of the Federal Election Campaign Act and amendments, but ruled that the FEC was improperly constituted. The FEC was reconstituted to conform to the Court's ruling, and in May 1976 it resumed its functions of enforcing the campaign finance legislation and dispensing matching funds for presidential candidates. Its political independence was still questioned by some, but its constitutional status was clearer.

1976 amendments were passed by Congress relating to receipt of federal matching funds and propriety of certain kinds and sources of contributions.

In 1977–1978 advocates of public financing sought, without success, to expand public financing to Congressional elections, as part of the Carter Administration's election reform package. A Senate filibuster by Republicans and Southern Democrats killed the financing part of the legislation in 1977. Republicans claimed the legislation was designed to help their future Democratic opponents, and Southern Democrats feared it would encourage Republican opposition in predominantly one-party states. A disappointed member of the Vice President's staff commented: "The only time you can bring about significant change is in the wake of scandal. That's how we got Presidential public financing."[3]

Restrictions

This section and the next on public financing provide a brief summary of the federal campaign finance provisions in effect as the 1970s ended. Candidates for the Presidency and the U.S. Senate and House of Representatives faced: (a) restrictions on contributions; (b) restrictions on spending; and (c) reporting and accountability procedures.[4]

1. *Restrictions on contributions*   The assumption behind these requirements is that wealthier individuals or organizations should not be permitted to buy potential influence with candidates by making large contributions. Thus, limitations nave been placed on how much individuals can contribute: no more than $1,000 per election to a candidate (1974 amendments); no more than $5,000 a year to a political action committee and $20,000 to the national committee of a political party (1976 amendments). The *Buckley vs. Valeo* decision permits unlimited

independent spending by individuals and groups, so long as this spending is not controlled by the candidate or coordinated with his campaign organization. Political action committees established by a corporation or labor union can contribute no more than $5,000 overall to a candidate in any election. Among other limits, limitations were placed on contributions to candidates by Democratic and Republican senatorial campaign committees.

Individual contributions to state and local races are limited by 22 states, and 13 others limit contributions by unions, corporations, or certain types of regulated or "privileged" corporations (for example, banks).

2. *Restrictions on spending*   On the assumption that extreme inequality in candidates' monetary resources will prevent the voters from being able to make a fair choice, a variety of limits have been placed on how much can be spent by candidates for presidential and congressional nominations and elections, and by national party nominating conventions. Media spending limitations, part of the 1971 legislation, were repealed in 1974, and the 1974 restrictions in turn were modified by the 1976 *Buckley vs. Valeo* decision. That ruling held that a candidate who refuses public financing can spend as much as he or she can raise. As noted, it also held that independent expenditures by persons unconnected with a campaign could not be restricted. Presidential candidates who accept public financing are limited to spending no more than $50,000 of their own or their family's money.

3. *Public disclosure*   The assumption here is that preelection public disclosure of the origin and extent of contributions to campaigns will provide voters with information that might influence their candidate choice. The corollary is that the knowledge that the information must be disclosed will discourage campaign organizations from making financial decisions that violate no law but whose propriety would be widely questioned. A wide variety of federal disclosure requirements were enacted in the 1970s, with enforcement in the hands of the Federal Election Commission. Some form of disclosure of contributions is required in 49 states, and 43 of these require disclosure before election day. Enforcement in half the states is the responsibility of a bipartisan independent commission and in half the states it remains the responsibility of the Secretary of State's office (the latter suspect in some quarters because it usually is an elective, partisan office). Reporting requirements have become sufficiently detailed as to be a major campaign task. Campaign organizations and political committees, for example, are required to keep records of contributions of $50 or more, and political committees also are required to report expenditures of over $2,000 to their stockholders or members. The costs of compliance with disclosure requirements rose to the point

where compliance costs had to be exempted from federal campaign spending limits.

Other than public financing for presidential campaigns, the reforms of the 1970s had the cumulative impact of limiting the forms and extent of permissible electoral participation. They reduced the manner and extent to which funds could be raised. (This was not unique to the 1970s legislation. Earlier laws had, for example, discouraged fund-raising from government employees, and equal time requirements discouraged provision of free broadcast time to major party candidates.) They also benefited certain kinds of candidates disproportionately. That is, the restrictions on contributions probably benefitted incumbents more than challengers, because incumbents are better known and do not require as much money to gain name recognition. Incumbents also have the advantage of being able to use office staff and other public resources in reelection efforts. The reforms reduced the advantage of wealthy candidates with networks of wealthy friends. The reforms probably helped Democrats more than Republicans, on balance, because of the relative success Republicans have had in raising money (thus having less need for public financing) and because the Democrats have access to organized labor's free manpower (which is not counted toward expenditure limits).

Public Financing

Candidates for the presidential nominations and the presidential nominees of the Democratic, Republican, and in some circumstances minor parties receive public funds. In the prenomination phase these are matching funds for candidates who meet the requirements discussed below. In the general election candidates who receive public funds may not raise funds privately. Eight states provide for public financing of specified candidates or political parties, and three states permit a surcharge to tax returns for campaign purposes. Fourteen other states permit a state income tax deduction for political contributions, and thus provide an indirect state subsidy. The state programs involve modest sums of money relative to the federal program, so we will discuss only the presidential financing here.

The assumption behind this legislation is that, if indeed contributions should be restricted, public funds are the only source of funds that do not beholden the recipient to some special interest. Some fear that public financing may increase the independence of candidates from the parties as well. To the extent that parties represent broader interests than do interest groups, it is argued that public financing may play a less liberating role than is assumed by its supporters.

The Revenue Act of 1971 first provided for public financing of presidential campaigns by allowing taxpayers to check off a dollar apiece on their income tax forms toward a general fund. Money from this fund is disbursed only in Presidential election years, with the 1976 campaign being the first with public financing. The 1971 act also allowed an income tax credit or deduction for contributions made directly to candidates for local, state, or national office.

Under the 1974 campaign act amendments candidates seeking their party's presidential nomination were eligible to receive matching public funds. To be eligible to receive these funds a candidate had to raise $5,000 in private contributions of $250 or less in each of 20 states. After meeting this eligibility requirement—designed to screen out candidates with purely regional followings—candidates received public funds on a dollar-for-dollar basis for all contributions up to $250 per individual. At the close of the 1976 nomination contests, Republican candidates Ford and Reagan had received almost $10 million between them in federal funds, and 13 Democratic candidates had divided approximately $14 million between them. Carter and Wallace were the major Democratic recipients, with more than $3 million each. One recipient (Ellen McCormack, $244,000) was not believed to be pursuing the nomination but rather was using the opportunity and funding to advance the cause of those opposing legalized abortions. During the 1976 prenomination period contributions from about 600,000 individuals (averaging $35 each) were used to obtain federal matching funds. Despite having had to suspend certification of matching funds for two months, the FEC distributions equalled 38 percent of total prenomination expenses for all candidates that year. In addition, public funding of up to $2.2 million was available for support of the national nominating conventions.[5]

The largest portion of public funds were reserved for candidates in the general election. The campaigns of Jimmy Carter and Gerald Ford received $21.8 million apiece in 1976, considerably less than the Democratic and Republican candidates had spent in 1972. In agreeing to accept public funds for their general election campaigns Carter and Ford had to agree to accept no more private contributions—other than $3.2 million each major party was permitted to raise and spend after the nominating conventions. This cutoff requirement makes the timing of the conventions more important than it was previously, since a candidate may continue to raise funds privately and receive federal matching funds up to the convention—even if that candidate's nomination is assured.

Any minor party candidate whose party had received between 5 and 25 percent of the vote in the previous election would have been eligible for these funds, and it was possible to become eligible retroactively as well if a new third party had polled that many votes. No minor parties qualified for public funds in 1976.

The implications of public financing are serious ones. In *Buckley vs. Valeo,* Justice Potter Stewart posed the question: Is money speech (and thus protected from regulation by the First Amendment to the Constitution)? The court did not give an unequivocal answer to this question because it permitted some restrictions on contributions and spending, while removing restrictions on candidates who do not accept public funds and on spending by groups not under the control of a campaign committee. Apparently the justices felt that First Amendment freedoms must be weighed against the presumed right of the voters to a relatively open election campaign. How can the financially limited candidate or party be assured a hearing from the voters without unduly limiting the right of any individual to make a political statement with money? This question is likely to continue to be addressed in the 1980s.

Public financing does not reduce the importance of campaign fund raising. Rather, it complicates the ways in which organizations must raise money and report it. In Congressional and state races in which restrictions on contributions have not been accompanied by significant public financing, the role of the campaign finance team is more important now than ever.

Finance and Presidential Campaign Organizations

The legislation of the 1970s has forced campaign organizations to make use of additional types of professionals, and it may have accelerated the trends toward expensive, candidate-centered campaigns. The legal requirements to be met in regard to disclosure and accounting for contributions have meant that lawyers and accountants, the indirect beneficiaries of so much federal legislation, are needed in campaigns as well. The requirement in presidential elections for candidates to reach more small contributors spread across the country makes it more likely that campaign organizations will require the services of direct-mail specialists, and entertainers and television specialists are needed for telethons. The telethon (a televised appeal, usually with a number of "guest stars," also used by charities) has been utilized widely in the past decade to raise funds for parties and political campaigns. Telethons have the advantage of attracting attention to the party or campaign, as well as raising money from across a large geographical area.

Direct mail has the advantage of permitting a more focused, single-shot approach, with appeals tailored to known characteristics of the recipients. Two of the best known direct-mail specialists are Morris

Dees, a liberal, and Richard Viguerie, a conservative. Alabama lawyer and former businessman Dees played a major role in the successful fund-raising efforts of George McGovern in 1972 and Jimmy Carter in 1976. Viguerie worked for George Wallace, among others. Three of the Presidential candidates most successful at raising funds through direct mail have been men with strong personal images supported by issue-oriented activists: Republican Barry Goldwater in 1964, third-party candidate Wallace in 1968, and Democrat McGovern in 1972. (Coincidentally, perhaps, though Goldwater and McGovern defeated prenomination opponents, all three lost the presidency.)

McGovern's fund-raising campaign began in January 1971, a year before the first primaries, with a mailing of 300,000 letters. Money is most important in the prenomination stage. Occasionally a major-party nominee, such as Hubert Humphrey in 1968, may have difficulty raising money. But, most commonly, it is in the prenomination stage, when a variety of candidates are battling each other and soap commercials for the attention of the public, that money tends to be most difficult to raise and most important if one has it. It takes money to raise money, so the lack of money takes on a self-fulfilling quality. McGovern and Dees secured large loans from wealthy persons (a practice now prohibited by law, if candidates are receiving public funds) to underwrite the direct mail drives. Some who responded to the appeals contributed on a monthly basis, and some had their contributions matched dollar for dollar by a wealthy contributor. Additional contributions were requested from the same people prior to key primaries—a practice also utilized by Dees and Carter in 1976. McGovern attracted more than 600,000 donors, and in the prenomination period raised $3 million at a cost of over $1 million. Most contributions were $100 or less.

As postal rates continued to rise, some feared that direct mail would cease to be a cost-effective means of raising money, but it was still being used with some success through the end of the 1970s. The Goldwater and Wallace campaigns had demonstrated that conservative candidates do not have to rely on wealthy contributors. The Goldwater campaign raised $5.8 million from 650,000 contributors. The Wallace 1968 campaign raised $5 million from 750,000 contributors. In the 1970s Viguerie became an essential part of many right-wing movements and candidacies. He could provide access to the names of approximately 30 million people who had contributed at some time to right-wing causes. In 1977, an off-year, he raised $25–30 million for conservative causes and candidates, but the cost of his services took the largest share of the amount raised. For example, in that year he raised $1.6 million for U.S. Senator Jesse Helms of North Carolina, but no more than $200,000 reached Helms.

However flush the organization, raising money is the aspect of the campaign most widely disliked by candidates and campaign managers, and subject to the most universal suspicion among voters. The same is true at the state level.

Money in the States

Money plays a role in state campaigns not significantly different from that in campaigns for national office. In state and national politics many businessmen and professional groups will contribute to the incumbents, but more tend to contribute to the Republicans, especially at the national level. Labor unions at all levels tend to contribute to the Democrats. People in industries and professions directly affected by state decisions are the largest contributors at that level. These include privileged businesses such as banks, utilities, businesses with liquor licenses, racetracks and other legalized betting establishments; the building and construction industries; and attorneys.

States vary somewhat in their campaign-financing practices. In Indiana the party in power assesses some state employees a percentage of their salaries. The openness of the "2 percent club" in Indiana is now unique, and even there the practice is being challenged. There commonly are state and local versions of the Hatch Act prohibiting such pressure on government employees and, as noted, many states have enacted disclosure, campaign expenditure, and financing laws of their own. Texas and Florida provide contrasting examples of the response of state officials to demands for campaign finance reform.

In Florida Governor Reubin Askew, running for reelection in 1974 with widespread public support, could have been assured an easy fund-raising campaign. However, feeling that the new public mood dictated it, Askew established a contribution limit of $100 per person. This forced his campaign workers to launch a fund-raising campaign more extensive than any seen before in Florida. Contributions were received from 8,876 people—large in historical terms, but still a small number in a state of 3.5 million registered voters. Texas, on the other hand, has led the nation in the number of contributors of $500 or more in state politics, and continues to require large investments for statewide campaigns. Governor Dolph Briscoe, for example, initially advanced his campaign $645,000 for his 1974 reelection campaign. Even candidates without serious opposition typically raise and spend substantial sums of money in Texas to promote them statewide for their *next* race.[6]

Candidates for substate and local office raise and spend far less than statewide candidates, of course. They use television less and inexpensive graphic arts more. They rely on volunteers rather than professionals. Table 5.1 lists the contributions, expenditures, and volunteer assignments for a successful North Carolina State Senate candidate

TABLE 5.1   Expenditures, Contributions, Volunteers for Democratic Primary Campaign for Kathy Sebo for North Carolina Senate, 1978

Expenditures

Radio advertising	$1,172.04
Cards and brochures	847.82
Newspaper advertising	636.98
Mailings	455.82
Fundraisers and receptions	407.23
Posters and yard signs	390.00
Bumper stickers	291.20
Photography	260.00
Stationery and envelopes	200.00
Campaign workshop	122.50
Telephones	91.72
Filing fee	48.00
Other expenses	97.24
Total	$5,030.55

Contributions		Volunteers	
Contributors	Amount	Telephone canvassing	60
		Pollworkers	60
22	$ 5 or less	Literature distribution	56
33	10	Addressing	22
33	15–20	Steering committee	18
39	25	Additional committees	15
31	30–50	Fundraisers	12
5	65–100	Staking signs at the polls	8
4	250–500	Drivers	4
Misc. change	16.74		
167	$5,317.74	Estimated total of 150 volunteers, some working in more than one area.	

Source: Senator Sebo Committee, Greensboro, N.C., unofficial report, May 10, 1978.

running for renomination in a county of more than 300,000 population. Senator Kathy Sebo won 13,960 primary votes at a cost of $5,030.55, or 36 cents per vote.

THE RESEARCH FUNCTION

The candidate must raise money. *The candidate must learn about the electorate.* This research task begins early in the campaign with research about the past voting habits of the constituency and its current attitudes and inclinations. The campaign organization must begin to develop information about possible issues and themes to be raised by its candidate and by opposing candidates. This work is an essential support function for the media staff, the issues advisers, the press secretary, and the workers doing canvassing, as well as for the overall campaign managers. The most important tool to gather this information is the public opinion survey or poll.

Opinion Polls

Privately commissioned opinion surveys are now used in almost all presidential and statewide campaigns, and in most congressional district campaigns and municipal election campaigns in larger cities. Usually, they are conducted by one of the more than 25 professional firms regularly doing such work, or in some instances by professionals acting as independent consultants or volunteers. See the "Polls" box for a discussion of how they are conducted.

Polls

Public opinion polling provides a practical method for ascertaining the attitudes and beliefs of large populations. By interviewing a sample of individuals, often comprising only a small fraction of the population, it is possible to obtain reliable information about the entire population. To do this, the sample must be representative of the population, which requires that the sample be selected by random procedures that do not bias the sample in favor of particular types of people. One common method is to randomly select households and randomly choose one individual from each selected household. Selected individuals are interviewed by a face-to-face or a telephone interview. The respondent's answers are numerically coded, and the survey results are processed and analyzed with the aid of a computer.

Despite the application of scientific methods, potential for error exists. A well-designed sampling plan may produce an unrepresentative sample, due to random chance and to the inability to interview every member of the sample (some will not be at home and others will refuse to grant an interview). Moreover, commercial polling firms frequently depart from a strict application of sampling principles in order to keep costs down. Even if the sample is highly representative of the population, there is the possibility that respondents may not answer the questions honestly and accurately. For these reasons, the results of an opinion poll are at best an approximation of the true nature of public opinion. Still, well-conducted polls provide a reasonably accurate picture of the population, and they are the best available means for studying the attitudes and beliefs of large electorates.

Opinion surveys published in newspapers or broadcast on television usually emphasize the "horse race" data from campaigns, that is, X is leading Y by 12 percentage points. Privately commissioned surveys provide a wide range of information other than who is ahead in voter preference at that time. The "horse race" data, if favorable, may be used in fund-raising to demonstrate either that the candidate has widespread public support or is gaining in comparison to an earlier poll. But to the campaign managers it is more useful, especially early in a campaign, to learn: What is your candidate's name recognition? What is your opponent's name recognition? What do respondents know about your candidate and the opponent(s)? What is the intensity of feeling, in support or opposition, expressed by potential voters? What issues do voters identify as most important?

Candidates may begin with low name recognition and poll support, and improve dramatically. In some cases, being an unknown may help a candidate, inasmuch as he or she has fewer enemies or unshakeable issue commitments. For example, when Dale Bumpers first ran for governor of Arkansas in 1970 he was an obscure country lawyer whose name was recognized by 1 percent of the state's voters.[7] But he went on to win the primary against a once-popular former governor, and win the general election. That year in two other Southern states candidates less widely known than their opponents (Jimmy Carter for governor of Georgia, Askew for governor, and Lawton Chiles for U. S. Senator from Florida) also successfully exploited the advantages of obscurity and overcame its disadvantages. Polls a year before an election are frames in a moving picture.

Increasingly, organizations in statewide campaigns will commission two or more polls, and it is the trends rather than the percentages themselves that campaign managers watch in the early and middle stages. The first poll will be more open-ended as the pollster and campaign manager search for the issues and themes that will strike a responsive chord among voters. Obviously, a candidate's past record and current predelictions will restrict the extent to which he or she can be packaged as a "fiscal conservative" or a "defender of the elderly," but even with a long-time incumbent it is possible to emphasize some parts of the record and play down other parts. Through multiple polls candidates can learn how voters are responding to their treatment of given issues or themes. The effectiveness and reach of television and radio messages also can be evaluated through use of poll data.

This type of research, like marketing research for a commercial product, attempts to probe for attitudes toward the product (candidate) among different sectors of the audience or market (electorate), so as to permit more precise focusing of marketing efforts on those sectors of the audience most likely to buy (vote for) the product (candidate). Such analogies, and the use of polling consultants and campaign managers, who in some cases also work in the commercial marketing sector, cause some observers to express the fear that the electorate will be manipulated rather than educated by a campaign. Certainly, the goals of campaign managers seeking victory and the goals of voters seeking information are not the same, but this was true in the prepolling era as well. Polling professionals say they merely try to do with precision what has long been done by hunches and experience.[8]

A second type of research, development of aggregate data profiles of the constituency using the Census and other sources, is in some cases done by party organizations and provided to the candidates. These profiles include demographic data and past voting records. Thus, these two types of research bring to the campaign managers information relevant to answering the following questions:

The office. What are the qualities voters seek for this particular office? Conceivably, voters may admire a candidate for qualities they feel inappropriate or irrelevant to the office being sought. This was true, for example, of many who leaned toward support of George Wallace in 1968.[9] Has the vote for this office in the past been larger or smaller than in other races held at the same time? Is this campaign likely to be affected by other campaigns of greater visibility?

The constituency. What does the constituency look like, in demographic terms? What is its political makeup: its voting history, party identification, registration and turnout rates? The campaign manager wants to know who and where are his "hard vote," the relatively dependable supporters of the party's candidates. Has there been a history of ticket-splitting or straight-ticket (party-line) voting? Census data, registration data, aggregate data from past elections, party precinct data, past canvassing records, and opinion survey data all may be used here to provide clues as to the likelihood of developing support among different groups.

The candidate. Do potential voters know the candidate's name? Do they feel they know something about him, and what is it? What are the personal qualities that appear to attract or repel potential supporters? Here the campaign managers are looking for candidate habits that can be changed, or for characteristics upon which political advertising can dwell.

Resources early in the campaign will be invested to increase the name recognition of a nonincumbent candidate, unless he or she is the relatively rare candidate (for example, a former public official, a well-known entertainer or sports figure) who comes into a campaign with high name recognition. Voters rarely vote for a candidate whose name they do not know—although occasionally they vote for a name they erroneously *think* they know. (See the box on "The *Other* Don Yar-

The *Other* Don Yarborough

The benefits of name recognition may have been demonstrated in the May 1976 Democratic primary in Texas. As voters were choosing Carter delegates over a favorite-son slate in the highly visible presidential primary (and another hard-fought presidential primary campaign was being decided on the Republican side), Democrats also were voting for a variety of state and local candidates. Midway down the ballot was a Texas Supreme Court vacancy. The only Supreme Court candidate who had campaigned significantly was Judge Charles Barrow, a Civil Appeals judge and the choice of every legal group that had taken a position. Also on the ballot was a man named Donald B. Yarbrough, to whom no attention had been paid by the press. For that matter, little attention had been paid to Barrow or to the race itself.

It is not clear what possessed the voters on election day when they got to that point on the ballot. Apparently many voters thought the Donald B. Yarbrough on the ballot was the Donald Yarborough who had been leader of the state's liberal Democratic faction in the 1960s and was a former candidate for governor. Another Yarborough (Ralph) had been U. S. Senator. Whatever the reason, Donald B. Yarbrough defeated Barrow for the Democratic nomination for the seat on the Texas Supreme Court. The Republican party having no nominee for the position, Yarbrough was virtually assured election.

The victorious Yarbrough revealed to a newly attentive press that the Lord had told him to run for the Supreme Court and had intervened to bring him victory. One editorial cartoon showed a voice from the heavens saying, "But I thought it was the *other* Don Yarborough!" It then became known that Yarbrough faced 16 lawsuits (most alleging fraud) growing out of his unorthodox business practices, and soon after he faced disbarment proceedings by the State Bar. A possible charge against him of attempted murder was discussed later in the press. Write-in campaigns failed in November and Yarbrough, already having lost the first of the lawsuits, was elected. In January 1977 Yarbrough took his seat on the highest court in Texas. Later that year he was forced to resign, and shortly afterward he was convicted of perjury and forgery.

The other Don Yarborough probably wondered where those voters were when *he* needed them. Despite his long prominence, he had never been elected to a major statewide office.

borough.") Survey data usually show that candidates, and the press, overestimate the extent to which voters know candidates' names and records. Statewide name recognition is often less than 10 percent for a city official, U. S. representative, or state legislator who has been active in political affairs for years.

The opposing candidate. Campaign managers want to know almost everything about the opposing candidate(s) that is known about their own candidate.

The issues.   How important do issues appear to be at this time, which are identified as most important by potential voters, and which ones cut across normal political groupings? The latter are issues that may attract to the candidate voters who by their socioeconomic status or party identification might be expected to support an opponent. What is the intensity of feeling about different issues?

Media habits.   When and how can different groups of voters be reached?

The campaign itself.   Multiple opinion polls are valuable because they permit managers to follow the progress of their campaigns. Polls provide information on the reactions of different groups to the candidate's issue positions, and the reach and effectiveness of messages sent through political advertising or direct mail. How are voters responding to opponents' campaigns?[10]

Information from a variety of public and private sources is integrated into a management information system (sometimes formalized, often not, sometimes effectively used, often not). This permits the campaign manager to select groups and localities for particular mass media, person-to-person, and candidate activities. Another responsibility in the research area is the development of information about issues on which the candidate will choose (or will be forced) to take a position.

Issues

The conditions under which issues appear to be important to voters, and for which groups they are important, were discussed in Chapter 3. Even the most pessimistic conception of the nature of the electorate grants that at least a minority is attentive, and that this usually well-educated and higher-income minority is interested in discussion of policy alternatives. Some voters are motivated by one overriding issue. Also important are the candidate's own campaign workers. Campaign activists tend to feel more strongly about issues and tend to take more ideologically coherent and extreme positions than does the mass electorate.[11] Campaign managers also recognize that it is usually advantageous for their candidates to be perceived as "facing the issues" because that is what members of the press expect. Candidates who refuse to discuss whatever newsmen believe are the issues may be labeled as fence-straddlers. Discussing issues will not guarantee a candidate space or time in the mass media, but most newspapers can find some space for candidate positions on the issues, even if it is not front-page space. In low-visibility campaigns, any news coverage is desirable, and discussion of controversial issues is a dependable route to such coverage. Interest groups that may support a candidate also demand that candidates publicly endorse their positions. An exception is an interest group, such as labor unions in many Southern states and the NAACP prior to the 1960s, that is strongly disliked by much of the electorate. These groups sometimes accept private assurances from candidates on the assumption that a public endorsement would hurt the candidate more than it would help the group.

Issues research usually involves the development of a series of background papers for use by the candidate, campaign managers, and speech writers. In some cases position papers also are developed and distributed to the press. These efforts require volunteers with special expertise (perhaps organized into formal task forces in larger campaigns). Their impact is seen in the seriousness with which the press treats the candidacy.

Issues research includes study of the opponent's record. Especially in campaigns against an incumbent, a campaign organization will investigate the opponent's official record (and in some cases, allegations of misconduct) to identify actions that could be used against him or her.

REACHING THE VOTERS

The candidate must raise money. The candidate must learn about the electorate. *The candidate must reach voters.* In the past three decades the ways candidates reach voters have changed as rapidly as any aspect of campaigning.

Television and the Press

The first time a presidential candidate visited 50 states, and probably the last time, was in 1960 when Richard Nixon did so. It was estimated that 10 million people saw him during that exhaustive, exhausting, and ultimately unsuccessful effort. That same year the average number of viewers for the Kennedy–Nixon television debates was 71 million, and national political broadcast advertising reached as many as 20 million viewers.[12] Personal campaigning by the candidate is essential because it is expected, and it is difficult to visualize even a twenty-first-century campaign without speeches given by live candidates in front of live audiences. But, increasingly, political campaigning at the national and state levels is being conducted through the mass communications media. And even personal campaigning increasingly means staged "media events" such as announcing a position on conservation while standing on the banks of an endangered river.

The increasing importance of broadcast advertising in campaigns has encouraged the candidate-centered, rather than party-centered, campaign. Television spots focus most effectively on a single person, rather than on an entire ticket. Party-line voting, on the other hand, traditionally has been encouraged through face-to-face contacts such as precinct work.

No area of campaign management is the topic of more folklore than the mass media. The image comes to mind of an inert voter/viewer embedded in an armchair in front of a television set. An unscrupulous media master has packaged the candidate into a "cool" image appropriate to television,[13] and our hypothetical voter/viewer is waiting to accept and absorb whatever he sees on the 21-inch screen. The process, unfortunately for campaign managers and fortunately for the American political dialogue, is not that simple. In using the mass media for political persuasion, campaign managers are competing for attention not only with the other candidates' efforts but with more pervasive commercial advertising campaigns. Political campaigns must reach people in a brief, intense period with a message relating to public affairs, a low-priority concern to most people, and must get their attention in the midst of situation comedies, war movies, rock musicals, and advertisements promising to make them richer, sexier, happier, better fed, cleaner, and generally more admirable. It is a difficult undertaking. We will examine their major choices in regard to media use.

How much to spend?   Buying media time is a large part of campaign expenses, especially for top-of-the-ticket candidates less well known than their opponents. If too much is budgeted for the mass media, other campaign activities will suffer accordingly; and if too little is budgeted, it may be impossible to remedy the error later. With funds insufficient to pay for reserved television spots in the 1976 Wisconsin Democratic primary, for example, Morris Udall had to relinquish the time. When the money became available, the time was no longer available. Udall narrowly failed to place first in Wisconsin.

What messages to convey?   The most important limitation on the ability of advertising specialists to package a candidate usually is imposed by the candidate him- or herself, inasmuch as the candidate is usually a person with a strong ego.

Which media are most appropriate?   Table 5.2 identifies advantages and disadvantages of the types of controlled media. Cost per individual contacted is only one of the considerations for campaign managers. Which kinds of people are being contacted is often more important than how many. For example, a Spanish-language radio station can be utilized to reach Spanish-speaking voters. Direct-mail campaigns, such as those used by the 1972 Nixon campaign to reach ethnic voters, also permit selectivity.

Since the 1930s radio and television have played important roles in

TABLE 5.2 Types of Mass Media and Their Audiences

Medium	Primary Goals in Using Medium	Audience	Cost
Display, e.g., billboards	Name recognition; advance themes linked to other media messages	General	Cost per individual contacted may be high
Other display and print, e.g., buttons, printed flyers	Stimulate & reassure supporters	Supporters; more informed audience	Cost per individual contacted may be high
Print, e.g., newspapers, magazines, direct mail	Reach selected audiences; advance themes linked to other media messages	More informed, higher socioeconomic-status audience	Cost per individual contacted is usually relatively low
Radio	Name recognition; advance themes linked to other media messages; reach selected audiences; introduce new themes in campaign (little lead time required); get out the vote	Commuters & other "trapped" audiences; housewives; youngest and oldest voters; ethnic groups	Inexpensive; much cheaper per minute than TV in time & production costs
Television	Name recognition; build an image of the candidate	Largest, least differentiated audience, including many with low interest in politics and some reachable through no other medium	Expensive

Adapted, in part, from Agranoff, *The Management of Election Campaigns*, pp. 336–337.

electoral campaigns. Radio follows people in their cars, to work, around the home, and in recreation. People do not make conscious decisions to attend to political advertising on radio; it is simply part of the sound environment. Some campaign professionals favor radio over other media, at least for local and state campaigns. Television is widely believed to offer the greatest opportunities for selling a candidate's image in a major statewide or national race,[14] *if* enough money is available. Television does have unique strengths; it permits persuasion simultaneously through sight and sound, and it provides the largest audiences. Television advertising seeks out voters, rather than waiting for them to seek political information, but this is true of several other media outlets as well. In some races television may be inappropriate: a local campaign in which little money can be raised; or a campaign in which there is little overlap between constituency and stations' audiences (and in which many of the viewers, therefore, are not potential voters). If political campaigns in New Jersey purchase New York City television time, for example, they are paying a price part of which is based on access to viewers in other states.

In most top-of-the-ticket races a mixture of television and other controlled media will be sought. Choices must be made not only between different types of media, of course, but within each type. For example, if an organization wants to reach lower middle-class housewives, time would be bought during daytime television "soap operas" and during evening programs with the desired audience.

Use of free media. The uncontrolled media can perform functions for the campaign organization that are difficult for the controlled media to perform even if ample funds are available. By uncontrolled media we mean the portions of news, public affairs, and entertainment programs and print space that cannot be purchased by advertisers. News and interview programs have credibility that paid advertising does not. That the time or space itself is free (in terms of direct costs) makes it doubly attractive for candidates without adequate funds to purchase time or space. For example, the 1970 Senate campaign of Lawton Chiles in Florida had little money to spend on the controlled media. Yet it was necessary to attract media attention, first to improve Chiles' name recognition, then to flesh out the candidate's image as an individual concerned about public problems. Chiles pledged to walk the quite considerable length of Florida. As he walked from town to town, he stopped at local radio and television stations to appear on interview or talk shows. The election of Chiles did not demonstrate the unimportance of the mass media, but rather the importance of skillful use of the uncontrolled media. Subsequently the campaign walk became a common device.

Most campaign rallies are scheduled early in the day so television news reports will be ready in time for the evening news. Some well-financed campaign organizations provide tapes and clips of their candidates for use on television and radio stations that are unable to cover campaign activities themselves. As well as extensive coverage, of course, campaign managers hope for favorable coverage.

When to buy time and space? These choices are partially determined by previous choices as to which media to utilize. Broadcast media often are employed heavily in the last weeks of a campaign, whereas display and print media tend to be utilized over a longer period.

Among the alternative approaches to buying broadcast time are: (a) a flat buy, with time purchased at a constant rate throughout the campaign; (b) an accelerated finish, focusing on the last two weeks of a campaign and increasing in frequency to a highly saturated finish; and (c) a spurt schedule, used early in a campaign and followed by the first or second approach. The first approach may be used to reinforce support for a well-known candidate. The second approach may be used by campaigns short of funds, and seeks to activate potential supporters and convert late deciders. This approach was taken by the Humphrey presidential campaign of 1968. The third approach may be used by candidates attempting to establish names and images in the minds of voters, and may be linked to fund-raising and other campaign activities.[15] A variation of the first approach was used in Edward Koch's successful 1977 campaign for the Democratic nomination for mayor of New York City. Media producer David Garth said he took an issues orientation to the prime time television broadcasts spread over the length of the campaign:

> It was a political decision. Ed [Koch] did not have the looks or the personality where he could go on television and say, "I love my country; now trust me." You had to make it issue-oriented. And I decided, do not buy heavy, buy long; buy over a long period of time. On television, Ed is the guy you have to see more than once or twice, and you have to have time to think about him in between.[16]

One of the most durable hypotheses relating to the mass media is that there is a two-step flow of information linking the media with person-to-person contacts. The linkage is from the mass media to opinion leaders around the country (or city), and from these individuals to the large network of people with whom they routinely interact on a personal basis.[17] According to this view, even a campaign fully committed to a mass media approach would depend ultimately upon person-to-person contacts, to be discussed in the next section.

Person-to-Person Contacts

Despite television and direct mail, people in campaigns in the 1980s will still talk to one another: in the early stages of a campaign, in canvassing and targeted voter registration activities; and late in the campaign, in canvassing and get-out-the-vote activities. The intent of these contacts may be reassurance, activation, or conversion of voters, to be discussed in the next section.

In a major campaign, because of the extent of mass media attention, voters cannot avoid encountering a variety of political messages. Voters tend to make up their minds earlier in high-visibility races—often before they are contacted personally. In this situation personal contact serves more often to make the campaign salient and to remind people to vote than to influence the direction of that vote.[18] Thus, a campaign organization often will canvass only sections known in advance to be made up of the kind of voters (for example, whites, middle-income) likely to support that organization's candidate. Incumbency, majority or minority party membership, and ranking in opinion polls also will influence choice of target groups. In a low-visibility race, on the other hand, canvassing may be one of the few occasions during the campaign when voters hear of the candidates in that race. Voters may be unaware not only of the candidates but even of the nature of the office being contested. In such races canvassing may lead to small changes in voter preference among canvassed voters.[19]

In the past local party organizations were responsible for person-to-person contacts. In the prototypical urban political machine the party kept in close touch with people on every block. Yet this was never true for all regions of the country, and it is becoming less accurate even for the older cities of the Northeast and Midwest. Studies from the 1960s showed that a quarter or fewer of the precinct organizations in one major city performed all three direct contact tasks (registration, canvassing, election-day roundup), and that county party organizations were less active the lower the office being contested. However, the percentage of voters in the nation who said they had been contacted personally by a party or candidate more than doubled from the 1950s to the 1970s.[20] This may reflect increased activity by candidate organizations—another sign of the current dominance of the campaign function by candidate organizations rather than by party organizations.

Whether done for candidates or parties, the bulk of this time-consuming, exhausting, and sometimes dull person-to-person work is done by volunteers. Table 5.1 showed that 150 volunteers were used in one state senator's primary campaign, for example. National campaigns such as Goldwater's in 1964 and McGovern's in 1972 that had highly committed partisans were able to work the "grassroots" vigorously. College

students have been utilized widely in canvassing. The value of organized labor to Democratic candidates lies not only in its financial contributions, but also in its selective registration and get-out-the-vote
campaigns and the volunteers it can enlist for other precinct work. John
F. Kennedy, in his campaign for the Democratic presidential nomination in 1960, used professionals to supervise building of precinct organizations, but this remains largely a volunteer sphere.

We have discussed several major tasks of campaign organizations—
the "how" of fund-raising, research, media and press relations, and
person-to-person activities. We are omitting discussion of another important task, campaign scheduling. The next section, incorporating several points made previously, describes the goals of the campaign, the
"why" of campaign organization.

PURPOSES OF CAMPAIGNS

There are at least five purposes of campaigns, the first two directed
at elites and activists, the last three directed at the general electorate.

Persuading People to Take the Campaign Seriously

The first purpose of any campaign is to persuade politically important
groups and individuals to treat the campaign and its candidate seriously. Early fund-raising is important not only for the money it brings
in but also because it signals to other potential contributors and supporters the candidate's strength. Efforts are made to persuade newspaper
and broadcast editors and reporters, by reference to the candidate's
past or present political strength, that the candidate should be given
space and time. Campaign managers try to persuade party and interest
group leaders that, even if they are unwilling to commit themselves to
the candidate when contacted, this is a candidate who must be taken
into account. A candidate who is not an incumbent, has not held high
office in the past, and does not have access to considerable amounts of
early money will have a particularly difficult task to persuade the press
and political leaders that he or she has a chance. Once politically influential people decide that a candidate does not have a chance (even if
they personally like or admire the candidate), this tends to have a
self-fulfilling quality. Candidates have won nominations without the
early support of politically influential people, but it is difficult.

Reassurance of Campaign Activists

This goal, in contrast to the first, looks inward. Part of what goes on
in campaigns is not designed to sway the opinions of political spectators.
Rather, it is designed to reassure campaign workers and contributors

that the candidate does indeed believe what they believe, and to reassure them that the campaign is active and prospering.

At every level parties and candidates develop platforms to run on. These compilations of policy positions are designed: (a) to help to persuade the press that the candidate is approaching the issues seriously, and to win continued press attention; (b) to show interest group leaders that their support has been (or would be) well placed, inasmuch as the candidate shares their views on important issues; and (c) to give campaign activists the feeling that they are working—almost always without pay, and often at some sacrifice—in a worthy cause. Most speech-making reaches relatively few voters directly, yet it is regarded as an essential campaign activity. The press expects it, the candidate wants to be doing something, and campaign activists want visible evidence that the campaign is on the move.

Some campaign funds may be spent as much to reassure campaign workers (and the candidate him- or herself), as to win support among the general electorate. In a contested top-of-the-ticket campaign an organization that spent little money—even if the candidate was heavily favored to win—probably would be one whose workers would feel anxious. Campaign organizational structure, too, may be most important for the morale of campaign workers.

Reassurance of Supporters

The last three goals of campaigns involve the general electorate. Early systematic studies of political campaigns, undertaken in the 1940s, identified these goals. One is reinforcement of persons already supporting the candidate—what we will call reassurance of supporters. The next is activation of persons who are potential supporters but are not yet motivated to the point of willingness to vote. Finally, there is the goal of conversion of voters initially opposing the candidate.

Of these three goals, reassurance of supporters occurs most frequently. In a 1948 study in Elmira, New York, 96 percent of voters expressing a partisan preference in August and October remained stable in their preference. The mass media (at this time radio and the print media) and the campaign itself served primarily, this study maintained, to reinforce the initial predispositions of voters. The reasons given were voters' selective exposure to information and the political homogeneity of the groups to which they belonged.[21] Voters, it was argued, selectively expose themselves to political communications (as people do to other kinds of communications), and pay far more attention to messages from the candidates they already are inclined to support. It was argued that voters also filter out information incongruent with their candidate preferences. That is, if their preferred candidate favors policy A and they favor policy B, voters may misperceive their candidate as favoring policy B too. Voters, furthermore, are surrounded by friends, relatives, and co-workers who share many of their predispositions.

Reinforcement, however, may have become less pervasive than it was in the 1940s. As partisanship becomes weaker, there are fewer voters with initial predispositions in favor of either party's candidates. Thus, there is less to reinforce. As television has come to play a more important part in campaigns, exposure to political messages may be less selective. Events such as televised debates have put both candidates in front of large audiences containing supporters of each.[22] As more voters are inclined to split their vote between both Democrats and Republicans,[23] they will tend to seek out messages from various candidates.

Activation of Potential Supporters

Some eligible voters may be inclined by party identification, demographic characteristics, or other factors to support a candidate, but may hesitate to reach a decision. One goal of campaigns is to activate these potential supporters, and get them to the polls. Developments in opinion polling have made it easier to identify potential supporters.

Conversion of Opponents

The most dramatic result of campaigns—conversion of voters from support of one candidate to support of another—was found in the 1940s to occur least frequently. In the last month of the 1948 campaign, for example, only 5 percent of the respondents changed their stated vote intentions.[24] Those who changed their intentions were those less interested in the campaign and less exposed to campaign communications—suggesting that the campaign organizations might not even be able to take credit for conversion of that 5 percent. Conversion may occur somewhat more often now than in the 1940s, but it probably remains the rarest of the general electorate impacts. And the stronger an initial commitment to a candidate, the less likely it is to be changed.

A related goal, although one whose attainment may be unmeasurable, is to mollify those opponents who cannot be converted. That is, a candidate would prefer not to be perceived by opponents as dangerous. A candidate perceived as dangerous is more likely to stimulate increased activity by the opposition.

This chapter has discussed the how and the why of campaign organization. The next two chapters look at recent experiences of campaign organizations in the two major phases of the electoral process: the nomination phase and the general election.

FOR FURTHER READING

Agranoff[25] is the best overall treatment of the hows of campaign management. Robert Agranoff, ed., *The New Style in Election Campaigns*, 2nd ed. (Boston: Holbrook, 1976) is a good collection of campaign management studies. Campaign manuals can be obtained from the Democratic and Republican national committees, as well as from various interest groups. Also see Marjorie R. Hershey, *The Making of Campaign Strategy* (Lexington, Mass.: Lexington, 1974). Alexander's *Financing Politics*[26] is the best summary of campaign finance. The best popular book on the press remains A. J. Liebling, *The Press* (New York: Ballantine, 1961).

NOTES

1. Marjorie R. Hershey, "A Social Learning Theory of Innovation and Change in Political Campaigning." (Paper presented at the 1977 annual meeting of the American Political Science Association, Washington, D.C., September 1977.)

2. William Endicott, "California: A New Law," in Herbert E. Alexander, Ed., *Campaign Money* (New York: Free Press, 1976), pp. 110–141.

3. *Congressional Quarterly Weekly Report,* August 6, 1977, p. 1692.

4. Figures in this discussion come largely from Herbert E. Alexander, *Financing Politics* (Washington: Congressional Quarterly, 1976); and Alexander, *Campaign Money.*

5. Ibid.

6. William Mansfield, "Florida: The Power of Incumbency," and Jon Ford, "Texas Big Money," in Alexander, ed., *Campaign Money,* pp. 39–109.

7. Unpublished opinion survey, WRH and Staff, Washington, D.C.

8. On polls see Charles W. Roll, Jr., and Albert H. Cantril, *Polls: Their Use and Misuse in Politics* (New York: Basic, 1972).

9. James Clotfelter and William R. Hamilton, "Wallace and His Supporters in Selected Southern States: Opinions and Behavior," *Politics 1974,* 3 (1974), p. 70.

10. Robert Agranoff, *The Management of Election Campaigns* (Boston: Holbrook 1976), Chapter 5.

11. See, for example, Denis G. Sullivan, Jeffrey L. Pressman, Benjamin I. Page, and John J. Lyons, *The Politics of Representation* (New York: St. Martin's, 1974), pp. 30–34 on activist–electorate differences; and Gabriel Almond, *The American People and Foreign Policy* (New York: Holt, Rinehart and Winston, 1950) on the concept of the attentive public.

12. Agranoff, *The Management of Election Campaigns,* p. 309.

13. The "cool"–"hot" imagery comes from Marshall McLuhan. See his *Understanding Media* (New York: McGraw-Hill, 1964).

14. See Joe McGinniss, *The Selling of the President, 1968* (New York: Trident, 1969).

15. Agranoff, *The Management of Election Campaigns,* pp. 348–349.

16. John Corry, "The Koch Story," *The New York Times Magazine,* October 30, 1977, p. 91.

17. Elihu Katz and Paul F. Lazarsfeld, *Personal Influence: The Part Played by People in the Flow of Mass Communications* (New York: Free Press, 1964).

18. Gerald H. Kramer, "The Effects of Precinct-Level Canvassing on Voter Behavior," *Public Opinion Quarterly,* 34 (Winter 1970–1971), p. 567.

19. John C. Blydenburgh, "A Controlled Experiment to Measure the Effects of Personal Contact Campaigning," *Midwest Journal of Political Science,* 15 (May 1971), pp. 380–381.

20. Samuel J. Eldersveld, *Political Parties: A Behavioral Analysis* (Skokie, Ill.: Rand McNally, 1964), p. 350; William J. Crotty, "The Party Organization and Its Activities" in Crotty, Ed., *Approaches to the Study of Party Organization* (Boston: Allyn and Bacon, 1968), p. 278; and Agranoff, *The Management of Election Campaigns,* p. 420.

21 Bernard R. Berelson, Paul F. Lazarsfeld, and William N. McPhee, *Voting* (Chicago University of Chicago Press, 1954), p. 16. Also see Lazarsfeld, Berelson, and Hazel Gaudet, *The People's Choice,* 3rd ed. (New York: Columbia University Press, 1968), dealing with a 1940 study in Erie County, Ohio; and Thomas E. Patterson, "Vote Choice in the 1976 Presidential Primary Elections: Issues and the Ford–Reagan Race." (Paper delivered at the Southern Political Science Association annual meeting, New Orleans, November 1977.)

22. See, for example, Burns W. Roper, "The Effects of the Debates on the Carter/Ford Election." (Paper delivered at the American Political Science Association annual meeting, Washington, September 1977.) The debates are discussed in Chapter 7.

23. Walter DeVries and V. Lance Tarrance, *The Ticket-Splitter: A New Force in American Politics* (Grand Rapids, Mich.: Eerdmans, 1972).

24. Berelson, Lazarsfeld, and McPhee, *Voting,* p. 16.

25. *The Management of Election Campaigns* (Boston: Holbrook, 1976).

26. Washington, D.C.: Congressional Quarterly, 1976.

CHAPTER 6

Nomination Campaigns

It was a bitter Democratic nomination campaign in Georgia in 1970. Early polls showed former governor Carl Sanders far ahead of his opponent, who had been campaigning around the state for four years. The former governor had the support of most of the state's business establishment and major newspapers. His administration had been unmarked by corruption—then an unusual phenomenon in Georgia. He had access to considerable campaign funds. His campaign theme was "Carl Sanders—Again."

Like many apparent winners in nomination contests, however, Sanders never made it. His own campaign theme—"Again"—labeled him as an insider in a period when many voters were inclined to vote against insiders. Sanders was a prosperous attorney. His opponent turned his prosperity, his expensive suits and private plane, against him. Sanders was identified as a moderate in race relations and a foe of George Wallace. His opponent took a studiedly ambiguous stance. Sanders had the support of powerful Atlanta interests. His opponent's campaign tried to turn this against him too with a populist theme reflected in this television spot commercial:

> "This is the door to an exclusive Country Club, where the big money boys play cards, drink cocktails, and raise money for their candidate: Carl Sanders." (Country club door opens; closeup of man writing check.) "People like us aren't invited. We are busy working for a living." (Footage of Carter talking with "average man.") "That's why our votes are going for Jimmy Carter. Vote Jimmy Carter, *Our* kind of man, *Our* kind of governor."[1]

To the surprise of many, Jimmy Carter won the gubernatorial nomination that year and the election, and went on in the 1976 presidential nomination campaign to surprise many more people.

In this chapter we will discuss how candidates are nominated. General elections determine who will hold government office; in most cases this means that the voters choose either the Democratic or Republican nominee for that office. One candidate is chosen from a field of two— an important choice but a narrow one. Nominations, by contrast, involve the selection by primary voters or conventions of one candidate per party for each office. This nominee is chosen from among those who had campaigned for the nomination, and those who had campaigned had in turn selected themselves from among the entire eligible electorate. Gubernatorial primaries, then, choose two from a field of perhaps several million people—and presidential nominating conventions select two from many millions more. Individuals can run for office as independents, of course, and have the prerogative of starting their own political parties. Maine elected an independent as governor in 1974. But in almost every partisan race in the past half-century it has been the nominee of the Republican or Democratic party who has won. This practice continues even in an age of voter ticket-splitting and self-identification as independents. George Wallace, after running unsuccessfully for President in 1968 as an independent, continued to run successfully as a Democrat in Alabama campaigns. In this chapter we will discuss the party processes through which the voters' ultimate choice usually is narrowed to two.

Some local elections, particularly municipal elections in the South and West and school board elections, are conducted on a nonpartisan basis.[2] Many local elections, virtually all state elections, and all elections for national office, however, are conducted on a partisan basis and thus require candidates to secure party nominations first. In states in which one party is dominant, securing the majority party's nomination may involve the only serious competition.

In the last chapter it was shown that candidates have been able to reach more voters in recent years with less mediation by others. Campaigns are increasingly candidate-centered, not party-centered. In the last chapter it also was pointed out that campaigns for top-of-the-ticket offices are beginning earlier, and requiring more money and professional staff. The growing use of primaries, and especially the growth of presidential primaries, has been an important factor. This chapter will elaborate on these trends as part of a discussion of nomination politics.

Several terms need to be defined at the outset:

Nomination: Designation of a candidate as the party's choice to run for a governmental office

Primary election voters
- (a) Open: Election open to any registered voter in the jurisdiction
- (b) Closed: Election open only to persons registered as members of that political party

Primary election (non-presidential): Popular vote to select the party's nominee

Primary election (presidential)
- (a) Delegate selection primary: State election of delegates to the party's presidential nominating convention
- (b) Preference primary: Nonbinding state vote to express preferences among presidential candidates, with delegates being selected separately
- (c) Unpledged delegate selection primary: State election of convention delegates pledged to no presidential candidate

Caucus: Lower-level party gathering, often to choose delegates to higher-level convention

Convention (non-presidential): Party meeting at state or local level to select delegates for presidential conventions, to select candidates for state and local office, or to conduct other party business

Convention (presidential): Party meeting to nominate candidates for president and vice president, and to conduct other party business

There are further variations and subtypes of the above, but this is sufficient as an introduction.

Presidential primaries differ significantly from other primary elections in that the former are stages in the nomination of candidates while the latter are themselves the nominating instrument. We will first discuss the non-presidential primary, proceed to a discussion of presidential primaries, and later in the chapter discuss nominating conventions.

PRIMARY ELECTIONS

State and Local Primaries

Political parties have been in seeming decline for years, and their death is regularly predicted. However, they continue to have meaning to many voters (see Chapter 3), and their nominations continue to be sought by candidates. In the past half century the typical means of conferring that nomination has changed: away from the party convention, apparently perceived as liable to boss control, and toward the

primary, with its presumed linkage to the ideal of an open and democratic nomination process. The party organization played a more important role in conventions, and advocates of strong parties continue to
favor selection of candidates through caucuses and conventions. Convention supporters point out that primary elections involve a variety of
costs and risks. These include increased financial costs to the candidate
organizations; the risk to society of discouraging or physically exhausting otherwise well-qualified candidates;[3] and the risk to the party that
a weak candidate might be selected inadvertently by the small, atypical
primary electorate or intentionally by crossover voting by opposition
party members. Despite these costs and risks, however, it is the primary
that is typically used now to nominate candidates for the U.S. Senate
and House of Representatives, the governorship, and most important
state and substate offices.

Primary rules are established by the parties, acting under state law.
Occasionally the federal courts have intervened in the administration
of primaries (for example, to strike down the all-white primary in Southern Democratic parties in 1944)[4], but this has been rare. To become a
candidate in a primary one must meet the legal requirements noted in
Chapter 4; file a declaration of candidacy with a filing fee by a specified
date; and, in some states, sign a party loyalty pledge. States have various
kinds of restrictions, and in some cases virtually no restrictions, on who
can cast ballots in primaries. In closed primaries only voters registered
as Democrats can vote in the Democratic primary. In open primaries
voters may vote in either primary, with the result sometimes being
widespread crossover of voters to the other party's primary. If the
leading vote-getter fails to receive a majority of the votes, a run-off
election may be held between the two leading candidates. If there is
no provision for a run-off, the candidate with the largest number of
votes (plurality) wins.

Primary elections are the ultimate in candidate-centered politics.
The party sponsors the tournament, but does not determine which
knights joust, nor which ones win. The trophy for the victor is the
mantle of the party, although the party organization has had little voice
in its award.

As noted in previous chapters, the primary electorate is smaller and
better informed than general election voters, and the advantages to a
candidate of money, media time, and name recognition are even
greater than in the general election.

The first consideration for any candidate is name recognition. In a
crowded field, without party labels to help the voters distinguish between candidates, this usually is the most important task for nonincumbent candidates. On the other hand, there are sometimes benefits to
obscurity. In some races it is helpful to be a new face free from the old

blood feuds of party factions and free of blame for current problems. Jimmy Carter was one of the "new face" governors elected in the South in 1970, and he also benefitted in the 1976 Presidential primaries from the ambiguity that surrounds a previously unfamiliar candidate. New York City Mayor Edward Koch started the 1977 election year known by only 6 percent of Democratic voters, but he won. Regardless of where candidates begin in name recognition rankings they hope, of course, to end the race with voters knowing their names and feeling they know something positive about them.

The larger the primary field, and the less well known the candidate prior to the campaign, the more important media attention is believed to be. A primary has features of the stock market; political activists want to support not only the candidate whom they believe is most worthy, but also the one whom they believe *other* people will support. It is the mass media that help potential contributors and campaign workers, and later voters, decide who is a serious candidate—that is, a candidate mentioned by and thus taken seriously by the media. The extent of press coverage a candidate receives may be more important than what the news stories say about the candidate; if a candidate had to choose between the two fates in a top-of-the-ticket race, being attacked by the press would be preferable to being ignored. Occasionally, in fact, candidates may even encourage press attacks. In the 1970 Georgia gubernatorial campaign Carter appeared to encourage the Atlanta newspapers to attack him.[5] The editorial and cartoon attacks on Carter not only kept his name in the papers but, given the traditional animosity toward the Atlanta newspapers through much of south Georgia, the attacks may have been doubly beneficial to Carter.

Presidential primaries operate under a unique set of procedural rules, to be discussed next.

Presidential Primaries: The Rules

The first state presidential primary to select national convention delegates was held in 1904. In recent years the presidential nomination process has been altered by the spread of primaries to new states— between 1968 and 1976 the number of primary states almost doubled, to 30—and by the adoption of new rules affecting delegate selection in the Democratic party. Rule changes are not tedious amendments of interest only to party professionals. They make things possible that previously would have been impossible or unlikely, often (as in 1972 and 1976) to the dismay of some party leaders. Some candidates are advantaged and others are not.

The period of rapidly changing rules in the Democratic party began in 1968, a year marked by public recognition by the United States government that the Vietnam War was unwinnable, by the pressured decision of President Johnson not to seek the Democratic renomination, and by the assassinations of two men capable of igniting great emotion (civil rights leader Martin Luther King, Jr., and Senator Robert F. Kennedy). It was not an easy year for the Democratic party to nominate a presidential candidate. Kennedy, brother of the assassinated President John F. Kennedy, had been shot and killed in the crowded kitchen of a hotel after leaving a celebration on the night of his victory in the California presidential primary. Lyndon Johnson was still in the White House and the war continued. The Democratic convention in Chicago attracted thousands of antiwar protesters intent upon making life miserable for Johnson's party. Protesters nominated a pig for President, then threatened to eat their candidate.

On one of the most tumultuous nights in the tumultuous history of the Democratic party, policemen and thousands of antiwar and anti-convention demonstrators became embroiled in a televised melee described by newsmen and subsequent investigators as a police riot.[6] The convention itself was portrayed by television as one in which Chicago Mayor Richard Daley, the last of the political bosses, ruled with a heavy hand and an obscene finger. The convention, it was widely felt, had given the party a poor image. After the defeat of its presidential candidate, Democratic leaders agreed that change was needed in the way the party nominated its candidates.

A Commission on Party Structure and Delegate Selection was established to propose reforms. It was headed by Senator George McGovern (not yet an announced candidate for the 1972 presidential nomination). The commission was told that the delegates to the 1968 and earlier conventions were too old, too male, too white. The commission recommended a variety of changes designed to ensure "fair representation of minority views." According to one rule change, blacks, women, and youth should be represented in each state delegation to the national convention in "reasonable relationship to their presence" in the population of each state. Significant for the subsequent nomination of McGovern were changes made in the procedures for delegate selection through caucuses and state conventions. Assuming that the McGovern commission had the correct criteria in mind, the 1972 convention clearly was more representative than the 1968 convention: the proportion of blacks, women, and persons under age 35 increased significantly. The percentage of women in the Mississippi delegation increased from 7 percent to 44 percent, for example, and the proportion of youth in the Tennessee delegation increased from none to 31 percent.[7]

Just as some Democrats interpreted the 1968 defeat as a reason for reform, some interpreted the 1972 defeat as evidence that the reforms (particularly demographic group quotas) should not be enforced with undue zeal. Probably more important, many state party leaders, believing that adoption of presidential primaries would remove any questions about the representativeness of delegate selection procedures, pushed for adoption of primaries for 1976.

Other practices of nominating conventions came in for criticism in the 1970s. One was the unit rule, whereby all members of a state delegation are bound to support the same candidate. Another was the winner-take-all system of allocating delegates to primary candidates. Winner-take-all (or plurality system) primaries magnify the importance of a state. California, for example, was a critical prize for Republican Goldwater in 1964 and for Democrat McGovern in 1972. The unit rule and winner-take-all primaries, like the Electoral College, emphasize the federal character of the political system and give greater influence to large units that become cohesive through the operation of the rules. Both tend to strengthen the position of party leaders within those state delegations.

For the 1976 primaries the Democrats, in the name of better representation of the average party voter and less boss control, called for proportional representation and selection of more delegates at substate levels. Proportional representation means that presidential candidates receive delegates in proportion to their share of the popular vote, as contrasted to the winner-take-all system. At least three-fourths of the delegates from each state in 1976 had to be chosen below the state level. The Democrats permitted two exceptions to complete proportionality and local orientation: (a) delegates could be chosen from areas as large as congressional districts, with the plurality winner at that level winning all of those delegates; and (b) to receive delegates, candidates would have to win at least 15 percent of the votes. Thus, small minorities would not be represented, presumably avoiding the extreme fractionalization feared by supporters of strong parties. Any electoral system exaggerates the share of seats won by the leading faction; the only question is how extreme the exaggeration will be. The Democrats reduced but did not remove this advantage for the leading faction.

States used a variety of delegate selection systems in 1976, with the largest number in both parties using proportional representation. Some states made use of the winner-take-all exceptions permitted by Democratic rules, some states retained nonbinding presidential preference primaries (so-called "beauty contests"), and some stayed with caucuses and conventions. The Texas legislature, to advance the presidential prospects of its U.S. Senator Lloyd Bentsen, adopted a primary law by which 75 percent of the state's delegates were to be selected from relatively large state senate districts. Balloting would be directly for delegate candidates, and the winner would take all. The primary worked exactly as it was intended to work—except that the beneficiary was not Senator Bentsen, but Jimmy Carter, who won 112 of the state's 130 delegates.[8]

Presidential Primaries: More Reform?

After 1976 various critics of the presidential primaries asserted that: (a) the primary season had become too long, and was now physically and financially exhausting for the candidates and emotionally exhausting for the voters; (b) atypical, small states had too much influence in the nomination process; (c) the increase in the number of primaries, and other forms of balloting and polling, had made it less likely that a clear choice would emerge; and (d) the primaries failed to account for voters' second and third preferences.

The Democratic National Committee in 1977–1978 attempted to deal with the first two objections by adopting rules to limit all stages of delegate selection to a three-month period (in 1980 beginning March 11 and ending June 10). Exemptions could go to states that opened their 1976 delegate selection process before March and were unable (perhaps due to Republican-controlled legislatures) to win approval of a date change from their state legislatures. Iowa and New Hampshire intended to retain their January and February dates in 1980. Under the current arrangement the New Hampshire primary is the first in the nation, and receives media attention disproportionate to the state's size. The state also benefits from a not inconsiderable quadrennial tourist boom, as newsmen wait to photograph the candidates throwing out the first snowball of the political season. Faced with the prospect in 1975 of losing its status as the first primary in the nation, the New Hampshire legislature decreed that its primary should be held one week before the primary held by any other state.

Critics of primaries concerned about the atypicality of Iowa or New Hampshire proposed a system of regional primaries in which all states in a region that wanted to hold primaries would have to do so on a specified date. This would put a candidate's showing in a small state in a larger perspective. On the other hand, it was argued that candidate support often varies by region, and that since momentum is such an important factor residents of the region holding the first primary would benefit. In any case, the Democrats did not in fact mandate regional primaries and did not prevent Iowa and New Hampshire from holding their early votes. Some argued that the changes would make Iowa and New Hampshire even more important by setting them apart from the blur of multiple primary results to follow.[9]

Critics concerned about the first three problems have advocated doing away with the present state primaries and national conventions and replacing them with two national primaries. However, this might

prevent candidates lacking national name recognition and major financial resources from entering the primaries and developing national
support. If the existing primaries fail to tap voters' second preferences,
the same problem would afflict national and regional primaries. In
circumstances in which there is not a candidate clearly preferred by
primary voters, conventions would be able to probe for the second
preferences of various factions.

The concerns that campaigns will become ever longer and that the
state primaries may not produce a clear choice are underscored by the
introduction of new polls and nonbinding votes. Parties in Florida and
Massachusetts scheduled nonbinding presidential preference conventions to be held late in 1979, before the first binding caucus or primary
vote.

The state primaries will be with us for the immediate future at least.
What the outcomes of those primaries mean, however, is far from clear,
and this will be discussed in the next section.

"Winning" a Presidential Primary

Identifying the winner of a presidential primary is a highly subjective
process. The candidate receiving the largest number of votes may or
may not be described as the winner by the press and political leaders.
If a plurality leader receives a small share of the total vote, this may or
may not be emphasized. The only concrete result of a primary is the
number of delegates won by each candidate; all else is interpretation.
The expectations set by the mass media, sometimes with the cooper-
ation of the candidates and other political leaders, are the hidden ruler
against which primary outcomes are compared. In New Hampshire in
1972 Senator Edmund Muskie had been expected to win easily, and had
reinforced those expectations by his own comments. When he won a
plurality but not a majority of the votes, the press described it as a
setback for his candidacy. The press characterizes vote totals as high or
low—but higher than what, lower than what? The origins of expectations are difficult to locate. They emerge from newsmen talking to
political figures and to each other and reading what each other writes.

When a candidate expected to win does so by a margin that reporters
feel is narrow, the candidate coming in second may be awarded a
"moral victory" and extensive press coverage. This happened with Eugene McCarthy coming in second against President Johnson in the 1968
New Hampshire primary, and with McGovern against Muskie in New
Hampshire in 1972. On the other hand, when the leading vote-getter
had not been expected to do well, the mass media may cover the
primaries on what amounts to a winner-take-all basis. This occurred in
1976. That year only the candidate who placed first in a primary, re-

gardless of the closeness of the vote or the impact on the delegate race, was given extensive press coverage. Narrow victories were exaggerated by the press to Jimmy Carter's benefit. Morris Udall, who placed second in seven primaries, received considerably less attention. One study showed that Carter received almost 50 percent of the press coverage given Democratic candidates during the early primary period, with no other candidate receiving over 15 percent.[10]

The next section examines the remarkable 1976 Carter campaign in more detail.

The Carter Campaign

At the beginning of 1976 no Democratic presidential candidate was acknowledged by the press and political leaders as the front-runner. The three best-known Democratic figures were Senator Edward Kennedy of Massachusetts, Senator Hubert Humphrey of Minnesota, and Governor George Wallace of Alabama. Kennedy, the last of the Kennedy brothers, had said he would not be a candidate in 1976 and appeared to mean it. Humphrey had said he would not be a candidate, although he was prepared to enter the race if no clear leader emerged. Wallace was unacceptable to most of the party leadership, and having been paralyzed by a bullet in an assassination attempt during the 1972 nomination campaign, he was not up to the vigorous campaigns he had waged in the three previous presidential election years.

Three U.S. Senators (Birch Bayh of Indiana, Henry Jackson of Washington, and Bentsen of Texas) and one former Senator (Fred Harris of Oklahoma) had announced for the Democratic nomination, as had two governors (Milton Shapp of Pennsylvania and Wallace) and two former governors (Terry Sanford of North Carolina and Carter). There was one U.S. Representative (Udall of Arizona), a single-issue candidate (Ellen McCormack, antiabortion), and a Kennedy in-law and former vice-presidential nominee (Sargent Shriver). Later in the year another Senator (Frank Church of Idaho) and another Governor (California's Edmund Brown, Jr.) entered the race. Jackson was believed to have access to the most money through his organized labor and pro-Israel supporters. Bayh also had labor support. Bentsen was believed to have some corporate support. Wallace had a proven ability to raise funds in small amounts. The new campaign finance laws meant that, to qualify for federal matching funds, a candidate would have to raise at least $5,000 in private contributions of $250 or less in each of 20 states. Reaching this level—as was done by all these candidates—was "a kind of license to practice," according to former Governor Sanford.[11] The availability of federal funds probably encouraged candidates to make the race who would not otherwise have done so, although it was believed at the outset that a candidate known only regionally (such as Carter) might be disadvantaged by the requirement that funds be raised in 20 states.

The Carter campaign,[12] planned by his staff and advisors since the 1972 presidential election, began in mid-1974 with small fund-raising efforts. Initial appeals were directed to friends and past contributors. The official announcement of candidacy in December 1974 was followed by the first large-scale fund-raising drive. Letters were sent to 30,000 Georgia friends and associates, and 500,000 names culled from lists of Democratic National Committee telethon contributors and 1972 McGovern campaign contributors. By the end of 1975, despite low name recognition in national polls, Carter had raised $850,000. Beginning in December 1975, and continuing each month thereafter, a Carter plea went to every donor of $100 or more, asking them to "double up" and contribute again. In the early stages fund-raising letters emphasized the Florida primary. One appeal asked for funds to keep Carter in the race to defeat Wallace in Florida, even if prospective contributors were unsure whether they preferred Carter to other candidates.

Through most of 1975 the candidates crossed the country to line up support, particularly in primary states, while their organizations visited national party leaders and newspaper columnists, local party workers and weekly newspaper editors. A Gallup poll in spring 1975 showed that Carter was the preferred candidate of 1 percent of Democrats. When Carter left the local newspaper office in an Iowa or New Hampshire town in 1975 to shake hands on main street, he had to introduce himself to everyone he met and explain that he was running for President.

As a largely unknown candidate Carter had to establish early that he was a winner. Thus, his efforts were directed at the first voting in 1976, the Iowa precinct caucuses, followed by the New Hampshire primary, and then the confrontation with Wallace in Florida. If Carter was successful in these, he expected that money would pour in; the leading vote-getter in a primary almost always enjoys increased support in opinion polls and increased campaign contributions. If Carter was unsuccessful in the early primaries, then the campaign was unlikely to survive until the late primaries anyway, so there was no reason to hold back money.

Candidates enter presidential primaries to demonstrate vote-getting abilities to others—party leaders, contributors, and voters in other states. Senator Estes Kefauver entered the Democratic primaries in 1952, for example, because he knew that his only chance lay with Democratic voters, not the party leadership. Although he led in 12 of 14 primaries he entered, Kefauver failed to get the nomination. John

Kennedy entered the primaries in 1960 to show that a Catholic could win—and was helped immeasurably by his success in heavily Protestant West Virginia. Richard Nixon entered the Republican primaries in 1968 to dispel his image as a loser—acquired through losing presidential and gubernatorial races in 1960 and 1962. Nixon had no significant opposition in the 1968 primaries, so he became a "winner" without defeating anyone.

Primary campaigns are not models of predictability. Past campaigns are studied in hopes of reducing the extent of the unknown, but sometimes the wrong lessons are learned and campaign managers—like generals—fight this election's battles with the last election's assumptions. The campaign managers of 1976 looked back to 1972 to draw their lessons. In 1972 Muskie had entered the primaries as the acknowledged front-runner. He hoped to do well in the first primaries to secure the nomination early. Muskie led in New Hampshire with 46 percent and in Illinois with 63 percent. The press said he should have done better. Wallace led in the Florida primary that year with 42 percent of the vote. McGovern led in the Wisconsin primary with 30 percent of the vote, after doing poorly in Illinois and Florida which he did not contest seriously. Yet it was McGovern's ranking in the national Gallup poll that increased, and it was Muskie who was described by the press as in decline. The lessons of the 1972 Democratic primaries, although muddied by the subsequent changes in delegate selection and fund-raising rules, were widely believed to be: (a) it is wise to pick and choose the primaries to contest, as McGovern had done, and risky to enter them all, as Muskie had done; and (b) George Wallace will continue to be a powerful force in presidential primaries, especially in the South. Carter's advisors initially read the same lessons in the 1972 results,[13] but later they concluded that Carter should enter all of the primaries; for a candidate starting with only a regional reputation this was necessary to demonstrate national support, as well as to pick up as many delegates as possible in the absence of winner-take-all primaries.

Fifty thousand Iowa Democrats (or 10 percent of the state's Democrats) voted in precinct caucuses, to be followed later by conventions that would select a mere 47 delegates (of the 3,008 who would be at the national convention). Because the caucuses were the first opportunity for people to vote—rather than simply express a preference as was done in Gallup polls—Iowa received intense media attention. The bases of the Carter effort were a 20-person state steering committee and a great deal of Carter's own time. The highlight was an effort to attract media attention by winning an informal poll of diners at a party dinner in Ames, Iowa. By getting his supporters to the dinner in great numbers Carter "won" the poll, and ultimately won 27 percent of the vote in the Iowa caucus elections. This was twice as much as any other candidate won, although it was considerably less than the uncommitted share. By winning less than 14,000 votes Carter had become—in the words of newsmen—the candidate to beat. Carter said later:

> The biggest problem I had was not campaign technique, or that I was from the South, or that I had not been in Washington, or that I didn't have any money, that I didn't have a good campaign organization—the problem I had was substantiality of campaign efforts in the minds of the people. Nobody thought I should be taken seriously. And we couldn't take any shortcuts to resolving it except to do better than we were expected to do in two or three of the states. We decided early on New Hampshire and Florida; later, we saw that Iowa was a good chance. . . . We just saw a good chance to build that up with a major media event.[14]

As noted earlier, the news media concentrated disproportionately on the leading vote-getter in the 1976 primaries, in part because Carter had not been expected to do well. Against the drawback of less name recognition for a candidate such as Carter must be placed the advantage of lower expectations by the news media. A candidate who starts low and improves is characterized by the press as having momentum. Carter's public recognition increased fourfold during two months of the nomination campaign, a California–Pennsylvania study showed, while no other candidate's recognition so much as doubled. By April 1976 Carter's public recognition in this survey had increased to over 80 percent, with no other candidate except Wallace being recognized by more than 50 percent of Democrats. People had to follow the news closely before they were likely to find Jackson and Udall familiar, but even the most casual news media followers felt they knew something about Carter. Of that survey's respondents who were *not* regular readers or viewers, 64 percent said they knew something about Carter— almost three times the percentage for Jackson or Udall.[15]

Following Iowa was New Hampshire, again a small state. Carter family members, "Peanut Brigade" teams of Georgians, and his state campaign organization contacted an estimated (by Carter) 95 percent of the Democratic homes in New Hampshire. As occurred at critical junctures throughout the campaign, Carter also was helped by decisions made by his opponents. Following the perceived lesson of McGovern in 1972, Senator Jackson had determined to pick his primaries carefully, and he had decided not to enter the New Hampshire primary. Carter was the only candidate not identified with liberal policies. Four liberal candidates together polled more than twice the number of votes Carter won in New Hampshire—but it was Carter who placed first and was on the television news programs the next morning. He had "won" New Hampshire by a margin of 4,301 votes over Morris Udall.

During the three months before the New Hampshire primary more than half of the campaign news on television dealt entirely or mostly with New Hampshire, according to one study. By contrast only 10 percent of news coverage was of the next week's Massachusetts primary[16]—with six times as many delegates at stake as in New Hampshire. After the New Hampshire victory, the Carter campaign redirected resources to try to win Massachusetts. Carter's own statements and those of his staff encouraged press expectations that he would do well in Massachusetts. His poll results had showed Carter doing well there, but his support did not materialize in the voting booths. It snowed heavily on election day, and this may have affected the Carter vote. (See box on "When Is Support Soft?") He finished fourth, well behind the leader Jackson, and this time a victim instead of a beneficiary of media expectations.

Carter's early successes made him increasingly the target of other candidates' criticisms. Carter was said to be vague on the issues. His speeches usually were full of details: from criticisms of Secretary of State Henry Kissinger (the ubiquitous White Rabbit of the Nixon-Ford administration), to proposals for government reorganization and tax reform. Yet the portions of speeches that people seemed to remember were less specific: his calls for a more honest government, "as good as the American people," and his call for more trust and love between the voters and their leaders.

After the Massachusetts miscalculation, the Florida primary was more important than it had ever been for Carter. Senator Jackson aimed only to win a few delegates in the Miami area. Still remembering

---

When Is Support Soft?

Soft support, widely referred to in campaign management, is difficult to identify in advance of a vote. Softness of support refers to lack of intensity of feeling. Voters may know a candidate's name and know enough about the candidate to vote for him or her if nothing else comes up, but it is not a deeply committed support. If other issues or candidates arise, or if external conditions (for example, the weather or family responsibilities) interfere, these supporters may not remain with a candidate or may not vote at all. Carter press secretary Jody Powell defined soft support in this way: "Soft vote is the voters who don't care enough to come vote for you in the rain."* Or, in Massachusetts, in the snow.

*Schram, *Running for President,* p. 38.

George Wallace's strong victory in Florida in 1972, the half dozen liberal candidates stayed out. Where Carter had been the only nonliberal candidate in New Hampshire, he found himself the only active nonconservative candidate in Florida. He attracted strong support among blacks, and used his Georgia supporters to work the other side of the state line to develop support among northern Florida whites. Carter placed first in Florida—less than 4 percent ahead of Wallace— but first. It was to be three months before Carter knew he had the nomination, but he had placed first in the three essential early races.

Carter placed second in delegates to a favorite son candidate in Illinois, and led Wallace again in North Carolina. Carter won some delegates in New York, although Jackson led there. The same day in Wisconsin Carter "won" that primary by a margin of 5,000 votes over Udall out of 670,000 votes cast. Udall had run out of money temporarily, or put it in the wrong state, and had to cancel a weekend of Wisconsin television advertising and a mass mailing. When primaries are decided by thin margins and the benefits of first place so far outweigh those of second place, there are many "what ifs" asked. For example, what if the two liberal candidates who had no chance, but received 13,000 votes in Wisconsin, had taken their names off the ballot? Would most of those votes have gone to Udall?

Jackson devoted major resources to the Pennsylvania primary in April, to demonstrate that he could win the large urban states usually necessary for election. Jackson's labor union supporters failed to deliver enough votes, however, and Carter placed first. The press implied that Democratic voters each time were speaking with a single, certain mind —choosing a "winner" for each primary—when many voters in fact were uninformed and undecided.[17] Although Governor Brown and Senator Church entered the nomination campaign subsequently, and each led Carter in more than one primary, the nomination campaign was all but over. With his leading vote in Ohio in June, Carter received the endorsement of Governor Wallace, Senator Jackson, and Mayor Daley.

Front-Runners and Challengers

Carter's success in the 1976 primaries was unique in the recent history of Presidential nomination contests. For the first time a party had begun the primary season without a front-runner (that is, a leading candidate) and ended it with widespread party agreement behind a nominee who would not have been nominated without the primaries. What other patterns of nomination politics can be identified?

The most common pattern has been for a front-runner to emerge by the beginning of the election year. These front-runners have a decisive

lead in public opinion polls; the support of party leaders; and the designation by much of the press as the most likely nominee. Of the '14
front-runners to emerge in both parties between 1936 and 1976, 13
were nominated. In those instances the primaries and caucuses around
the country simply confirmed what the press and polls had already
"announced": that candidate X was the choice of his party. Only in the
Democratic campaign of 1972 did a clear front-runner (Senator Muskie)
fail to win the nomination. Four times the year began with close two-
candidate races: the Republicans in 1948, 1952, 1964, and 1976. In each
case the nomination period ended with the candidates almost as close
as they were at the beginning of the year. Three times (Republicans in
1940, Democrats in 1952 and 1968) a candidate was nominated without
having participated in any primaries. Much heat was generated by
some of these primaries. There were lively battles involving, for example, Senator Robert A. Taft and General Dwight D. Eisenhower in 1952
(Republicans); Senators John F. Kennedy and Hubert H. Humphrey in
1960 (Democrats); and Senators Robert F. Kennedy and Eugene
McCarthy in 1968 (Democrats). But in 20 (of the last 22) nomination
contests the primaries were not decisive in determining the outcome.[18]

The two exceptions were in the 1972 and 1976 Democratic nomination campaigns. In 1972 Senator McGovern started far behind front-
runner Muskie in the polls, ran surprisingly (surprising, that is, to the
press and party leaders) well in the primaries and caucus battles, and
ultimately won the nomination. In 1976, with no clear front-runner at
the beginning of the year, more than a dozen candidates entered one
or more of the Democratic primaries, with Carter ultimately winning
the nomination. Only in these two instances were candidates nominated who were unlikely to have won if there had not been primaries.
Whereas primaries most commonly have left party consensus or division as it was at the beginning of the election year, in 1976 the primaries
helped to create consensus behind Carter where none previously existed.[19]

An incumbent President has not been denied renomination by his
party since 1884, although Presidents Truman and Johnson (both in the
midst of war problems) chose not to seek another term. The strongest
challenge since 1912 to an incumbent President seeking renomination
occurred in 1976 when former Governor Ronald Reagan challenged
President Gerald Ford for the Republican nomination. Ford and Reagan started the year close in the opinion polls, divided the primaries,
and ultimately Ford was renominated by a margin of only 1,187 to
1,070 delegate votes. This campaign suggests that in the future incumbents may have more difficulty being renominated. Changes in party
rules and campaign financing laws have encouraged more candidates
to run in recent years, and some national problems may be difficult for

any President to solve. On the other hand, if Ford had not been the incumbent, it is difficult to imagine him defeating Reagan. Ford was the only President who never had been elected to national office,[20] and Reagan was a well-known former movie actor regarded as a skillful campaigner.

Primaries serve purposes other than selecting and affecting delegates. They also are a means through which voters express discontent by voting for protest candidates without the risk that the protest candidate will thereby hold any office. Voting for George Wallace in the 1964 and 1972 Democratic primaries permitted voters unhappy with civil rights and other national policies to "send them a message," as Wallace's 1972 campaign theme suggested.

Thus, front-runners with commanding leads at the beginning of an election year usually win, and many incumbents have been front-runners. But recent presidential nomination campaigns give no cause for complacency to front-runners and incumbents. The experiences of 1972 and 1976 show the unreliability of traditional expectations in periods of rapid change.

Several candidates have stayed out of the primaries and yet been nominated, which suggests that in rare circumstances the party leaders may still be able to choose their nominee. The forum in which this choice is made is the national nominating convention, to be discussed in the next section.

PRESIDENTIAL NOMINATING CONVENTIONS

Each of the national parties comes together once, or at most twice, every four years. Each party has a national committee and party chairperson to conduct party business between conventions, but it is usually only in the national nominating conventions in the summer of presidential election years that a large number of party representatives come together. (In the 1970s, the Democratic party also held two conferences in even-numbered non-presidential-election years. These conferences made decisions on party rules and passed resolutions.) Approximately 2,000–3,000 delegates (the number varying by party and by year), plus alternate delegates, gather for the main purpose of selecting presidential and vice presidential nominees. The nominating convention has been a grand (if not always honored) tradition in American politics since the 1830s–1840s. Its parades and balloons, its full auditoriums and empty speeches sometimes have seemed designed to persuade the electorate that neither party is sober enough to entrust with the leadership of the country. On some occasions the conventions, deadlocked, have had to rely on bargaining among party leaders in a "smoke-filled room"[21] to choose a candidate. An extreme case was the 1924 Democratic convention that took 103 ballots to choose a nominee (John W. Davis), who was not among the top three candidates until late in the balloting. That convention prompted the cynical journalist H. L. Mencken to observe:

> Herein, indeed, lies the chief merit of democracy, when all is said and done; it may be clumsy, it may be swinish, it may be unutterably incompetent and dishonest, but it is never dismal—its processes, even when they irritate, never actually bore.... The essence of comedy was here. And a moral lesson no less, to wit the lesson that it is dangerous, in politics, to be too honest. The Honorable Mr. Davis won the nomination by dodging every issue that really stirred the convention. The two factions lost everything that they had fought for. It was as if Germany and France, after warring over Alsace-Lorraine for centuries, should hand it over to England.[22]

Whether changes since 1924 would prompt Mencken, were he still alive, to judge democracy to be any less incompetent and dishonest, cannot be said. It is almost certain, however, that he would find national conventions less amusing. They have been streamlined for television's start-to-finish coverage. The speeches have been reduced in number, the parades curtailed, and events scheduled to reach a maximum evening audience of television viewers.

Nomination conflicts, such as the one Mencken described, now tend to be settled prior to the convention. Between 1956 and 1976 neither party required more than one ballot to choose a presidential nominee. The primaries have taken over a function previously performed by convention balloting, that of informing delegates of the relative strength of the candidates. Delegates who have not yet made up their minds can look at early primary results instead of having to wait for the early convention ballots. As a result, party leaders and delegates are being pressured by candidates to make their decisions sooner than in the past. Instead of being the scene of bargaining among state parties, as fairly cohesive units, the nominating conventions in recent years have been ratifying the preferences expressed by the primary electorate or by party leaders even before the primary season.

Other means of reducing uncertainty for delegates are procedural and platform motions prior to candidate balloting at the convention. One such vote occurred when the 1972 Democratic convention voted to overturn a credentials committee ruling to reapportion the California delegation. The controversy, brought to the courts by McGovern's opponents, had been returned by the U.S. Supreme Court to the convention for decision. The credentials committee decision, if upheld, would have stripped McGovern of 151 of the 271 delegates he had won in California, and would have been a signal to wavering delegates that his nomination was not assured. Prior to the 1976 Republican convention candidate Reagan had revealed his vice presidential choice, if he were nominated. Ford declined to do so. Voting on a Reagan motion to compel presidential candidates to reveal their vice presidential choices in advance was an indicator of the strength of the two factions. Ford won the procedural vote narrowly, as he did the nomination.

The conventions, then, are the scenes of important test votes, and might in the future again have multiballot candidate voting as well.[23] Several hypothetical situations might lead to a convention decision not obvious beforehand: if a beloved party figure had chosen not to enter the primaries; if the leader in primary results was completely unacceptable to important party factions; if, in a two-candidate race, a third candidate held tightly to a small number of votes, denying either of the other candidates the necessary absolute majority.

Even if multiballot voting does not return, the conventions have the potential to play an important role in promoting party unity or in deciding that other goals are more important than unity. Who are the delegates who will make these choices, and from where do they come?

Prior to 1912 delegates were apportioned among the states in rough accord with population. Often, and most conspicuously in the 1912 Republican convention that renominated William H. Taft over former President Theodore Roosevelt, this meant that delegates from states in which the party was weak (in this case Southern states) were controlled by the national party leadership. To ensure that states with strong parties were fairly represented, both parties subsequently added bonus votes to reflect past partisan strength. Thus, states that had voted for the party's candidate in the previous presidential election, or in some instances had elected party candidates for other major offices, would receive additional delegates at the convention.

In the past decade both parties have changed significantly their apportionment systems for delegates. The Democrats after 1968 used a formula that gave weight to a state's population and to its past Democratic vote. Electoral victory as such is not rewarded in this system, which tends to reward larger, more competitive, and more "liberal" states. On the other hand, the Republican system favors smaller, Republican-voting, and more "conservative" states.[24] This is accomplished by awarding bonus delegates in approximately equal numbers to states won by Republicans, regardless of the state's population. Through this system states in the South, Southwest, and Far West have been gaining Republican delegates at the expense of the older sections of Republican strength in the Northeast and Midwest. Population shifts to the "Sunbelt," of course, have accentuated this trend. A hypothetical recasting of the 1976 Republican convention voting using 1952 allocations of delegates by states suggests that Ford would have won 56 percent of the votes if allocations had been left alone, rather than the 51 percent he actually won.[25]

Traditionally, convention delegates have been disproportionately white, male, middle-aged, and high in social status. The impact of the McGovern Commission rule changes on the composition of the 1972 Democratic convention has been noted. The proportion of black, female, and under-30 delegates rose significantly. Amateurism also has been identified as an important delegate characteristic. Between 1944 and 1968 slightly less than two-thirds of convention delegates had not attended previous conventions. In 1972, by contrast, the proportion of Democratic delegates attending their first convention was 84 percent. The convention amateur tends to be a political purist interested in a candidate's issue positions rather than in his ability to unify the party and win the election.[26] In 1964 Goldwater supporters, including many amateurs, booed Goldwater's former rival Nelson Rockefeller even after the outcome was assured, and helped to set the tone for a convention that further divided the party.

Sometimes, as with some of Goldwater's supporters, a party faction will be more interested in nominating its candidate than in winning the election to follow. More commonly, candidates try to choose a convention strategy that does not preclude a successful election campaign. A divided convention does not necessarily spell electoral defeat; it depends on the party's circumstances. High levels of convention conflict are inversely related to November popular votes for parties that already hold the White House. (In this situation conflict may reflect unhappiness with the incumbent.) But for "out" parties high levels of convention conflict are positively related to popular votes in November. In this case convention conflict may reflect the fact that widespread expectations of electoral success have encouraged a number of candidates to seek the nomination.[27]

Because of Carter's early victories, and the collapse of most of his opposition before the convention began, the 1976 Democratic convention was less divided than many "out" party conventions are. The party left the convention in a relatively unified spirit, contrasted with the divisive Democratic conventions of 1968 and 1972. Conventions provide various opportunities to placate the disappointed. For example, a vice presidential nominee can be chosen to appeal to a faction that did not win the presidential nomination. Both vice presidential nominees in 1976 served this purpose. Platform promises are another type of "side payment" to a losing faction.

With candidates nominated, and losing factions hopefully placated, the parties now turn to the general election campaign, to be discussed in the next chapter.

FOR FURTHER READING

For an examination of the different patterns of presidential nomination campaigns and convention decisions, see Keech and Matthews, *The Party's Choice.*[28] A large number of journalistic accounts exist for particular presidential races, including Theodore H. White, *The Making of the President, 1960* (New York: Pocket Books, 1961) and subsequent versions for 1964, 1968, and 1972, and Schram, *Running for President* [29] on the Carter campaign. The literature on state and substate races is less extensive. See Alan L. Clem with associates, *The Making of Congressmen: Seven Campaigns of 1974* (North Scituate, Mass.: Duxbury Press, 1976). Sullivan et al.[30] is a study of the delegates to the 1972 Democratic national convention. On political parties see the review essay by James Clotfelter, "The Future of Political Parties as Organizations and Symbols," *Public Administration Review*, 35 (September–October 1975), pp. 554–559.

NOTES

1. James Clotfelter and William R. Hamilton, "Electing a Governor in the Seventies," in Thad Beyle and J. Oliver Williams, Eds., *The American Governor in Behavioral Perspective* (New York: Harper, 1972), p. 34.

2. See Willis Hawley, *Nonpartisan Elections and the Case for Party Politics* (New York: Wiley, 1973).

3. In 1975 Senator Walter Mondale withdrew from the 1976 Democratic presidential nomination campaign. He said he did not "have the overwhelming desire to be president which is essential for the kind of campaign that is required" (*Congressional Quarterly Weekly Report*, November 30, 1974, p. 3214). He said he was not willing to stay in Holiday Inn motels for two years. Some observers have asked whether the primary system forces candidates to surround themselves with relatively inexperienced staff members who can afford to spend two years in a gamble to reach the White House; it has been suggested that such staff members may not be suited to policy responsibilities in the White House. The possible hazards of staffing an administration with campaign workers are not unique to the federal government, however.

4. *Smith vs. Allwright,* U.S. Supreme Court, 1944.

5. Clotfelter and Hamilton, "Electing a Governor . . . ," p. 37.

6. Viewers did not interpret events in the same way. J. P. Robinson, "Public Reaction to Political Protest: Chicago, 1968," *Public Opinion Quarterly*, 34 (Spring 1970), pp. 1–9.

7. Denis G. Sullivan, Jeffrey L. Pressman, Benjamin I. Page, and John J. Lyons, *The Politics of Representation* (New York: St. Martin's Press, 1974), pp. 17–18; Gerald M. Pomper, "New Rules and New Games in the National Conventions" (Paper delivered at

the American Political Science Association annual meeting, Washington, September 1977 p. 7); and Glen Browder, "The Reform Experience" (Paper delivered at the Southern Political Science Association annual meeting, Atlanta, November 1973) p. 8.

8. Pomper, "New Rules and New Games ...," pp. 8, 10, Table 4.

9. *Congressional Quarterly Weekly Report,* June 16, 1979, p. 1170.

10. Thomas E. Patterson, "Press Coverage and Candidate Success in Presidential Primaries: The 1976 Democratic Race" (Paper delivered at the American Political Science Association annual meeting, Washington, September 1977) p. 3.

11. Herbert E. Alexander, *Financing Politics* (Washington: Congressional Quarterly 1976), p. 253.

12. Martin Schram, *Running for President* (New York: Pocket Books, 1976) is a good description of the Carter campaign and is a source for the following discussion.

13. Schram, *Running for President,* p. 66. Also see Gerald Pomper, *The Election of 1976* (New York: McKay, 1977), pp. 8–9.

14. Schram, *Running for President,* pp. 7–8.

15. Patterson, "Press Coverage and Candidate Success ...," pp. 8–9.

16. Michael T. Robinson and Karen A. McPherson, "For Better or Worse, News Content Can Make a Difference," unpublished paper, 1976, cited in Patterson, "Press Coverage and Candidate Success ...," p. 5.

17. Patterson, "Press Coverage and Candidate Success ...,"p. 13.

18. William R. Keech and Donald R. Matthews, *The Party's Choice* (Washington: Brookings Institution, 1976); and Keech, "The 1976 Presidential Nominations in the Context of the Previous Twenty" (Paper delivered at the American Political Science Association annual meeting, Chicago, September 1976).

19. Keech, "The 1976 Presidential Nominations ...," p. 9.

20. When Nixon was reelected in 1972 his Vice President was Spiro Agnew. A bribery scandal from his earlier administration as governor of Maryland led Agnew to resign. Nixon then selected U.S. Representative Ford as his new Vice President. When Nixon resigned in 1974 (see "Watergate" box in Chapter 5), Ford became President. Thus, Ford had not run for national office before 1976.

21. The term was coined by a supporter of Warren G. Harding, the Republican presidential nominee in 1920.

22. Malcolm Moos, Ed., *H. L. Mencken on Politics* (New York: Vintage, 1960), p. 84. Whether because of apprehensions about possible "smoke-filled room" decisions or for other reasons, public suspicion of conventions remains. In a 1976 Gallup poll 68 percent of the respondents favored nationwide primary elections, with only 21 percent supporting continuance of the nominating conventions. W. Ross Brewer and Garrison Nelson,

"Convention Conflict and Election Outcomes, 1840–1976" (paper delivered at the American Political Science Association annual meeting, Chicago, September 1976) p. 90.

23. Most delegates are bound, by public expectation if not by law, to vote for the candidate to whom they are pledged on the first one or two ballots, or until they are released by the candidate.

24. Pomper, "New Rules and New Games. . . . ," pp. 22–25.

25. Pomper, "New Rules and New Games. . . . ," p. 23. Conventions reflect all biases in the allocation of delegates to primary contestants, most conspicuously the bias in all systems favoring the candidate who places first. In 1972 McGovern won 25 percent of the aggregate popular vote in the primaries and 60 percent of the delegates from primary states. Democratic rule changes abolished the unit rule and weakened the winner-take-all provisions, but Carter in 1976 continued to benefit from a slight bias in favor of the plurality winner. If all states had employed statewide proportional representation with no minimum quota, for example, Pomper (Tables 3–4, p. 17) hypothesizes that Carter would have won only 36 percent (versus almost 42 percent in fact) of the delegates in primaries. Even such a small difference conceivably could have changed the behavior of contributors, delegates, and party leaders sufficiently to alter the outcome of the nomination battle. One change that clearly benefitted Carter was the addition of new state primaries. He won nearly two-thirds of the delegates from the 13 states that added primaries between 1972 and 1976.

26. Sullivan et al., *The Politics of Representation,* pp. 23–24, 124–125; and John Soule and James Clarke, "Amateurs and Professionals: A Study of Delegates to the 1968 Democratic National Convention," *American Political Science Review,* 64 (September 1970), pp. 888–899. Convention amateurs are not necessarily political amateurs, as Sullivan et al. demonstrate, p. 24.

27. Brewer and Nelson, "Convention Conflict . . . ," p. 6. Also see Keech and Matthews, *The Party's Choice,* Chapter 6.

28. Washington, D.C.: Brookings Institution, 1976.

29. New York: Pocket Books, 1976.

30. *The Politics of Representation* (New York: St. Martin's, 1974).

CHAPTER 7

The General Election

We come now to the final stage in the campaign process—the general election. This is the stage at which maximum press and public attention is focused on the (usually) two candidates remaining in the race for each office. With the party nomination in hand, the candidate will change his or her approach, although the candidate organization still will have to do most of the campaign work.

The party nomination provides psychological cues to the voters, brings new financial assistance, and ensures one's name being on the ballot. The importance of the latter benefit was underscored by the enormous effort and expense required to place the American Independent Party's candidates for President and Vice President (George Wallace and Curtis LeMay) on the ballot in every state in 1968.[1] Instead of seeking to differentiate himself or herself from other members of the same party, the newly nominated candidate in many cases now will try to minimize these differences and to stress the continuities that link him or her with Franklin Roosevelt (Democrat) or Abraham Lincoln (Republican). (Republicans, especially Southern Republicans, are less likely to stress party.) Whereas primaries are characterized by the lack of party cues to guide voters, party now becomes a factor for voters. If raising enough money was a problem before the primary, it usually becomes less troublesome afterward.[2] Either public financing will be available (for presidential candidates) or the normal sources of party financial support (including elements that supported other candidates in the prenomination stage) will come forward to help the nominee. The extent to which the latter occurs depends on the seriousness of divisions created by the nomination struggle. The problem of inadequate name recognition is reduced by a nomination victory, although nominees for lower-level offices still may arrive at election day known by name to only a minority of the voters. The voters will differ from primary campaign voters, too. A larger share of the potential electorate must be reached for the general election, as turnout will be higher. The new target audiences for campaign appeals will tend to be less educated, lower in other class measures, and less politically interested and knowledgeable. More of the campaign messages will have to find the potential voters, rather than vice versa. This will affect relative use of the mass media and person-to-person activities. The overall campaign strategy will change, and campaign managers may attempt to change the style of the candidate to adjust to the new situation. For example, candidates who refrained from criticizing their opponents in the primaries are unlikely to do so in the general election.

Reaching the right people at the right time is what campaigns are about, so timing is an important problem in the general election. Most eligible voters spend most of their waking hours thinking of things other than politics. It is only sporadically, and then often grudgingly, that most voters bring themselves to consider politics and political candidates.

No study has yet determined when voters actually make their choices. Voters have been asked this question regularly, of course, but unlike most of the information that polls seek from people, information about when a voting decision was made may be psychologically inaccessible to the respondents. The voter may really not know when his or her choice was made.[3] National survey data have shown that approximately two-thirds of respondents say they have made their general election presidential candidate choice by the end of the nominating conventions. Another fifth makes its decision after the conventions but prior to the last two weeks of the campaign. Slightly more than a tenth say they make their choices within two weeks of the election, with some of these deciding on election day. In a year in which the two nominees are well known, such as in 1956 when President Eisenhower and Adlai Stevenson were opposing each other for the second time, a larger percentage of voters say they decide by the end of the conventions. A year of turmoil and uncertainty, such as 1968 when a third party candidate was running, finds more voters waiting until late in the campaign to decide, and finds candidate choice less stable.[4]

Due to the lesser interest in and information about such races, one expects (but cannot prove, due to lack of data) voters to make decisions in the bottom-of-the-ticket races later in the campaign. Some campaign managers in bottom-of-the-ticket races believe that it is hopeless to try to get voters' attention until the last two weeks.

As much as any other factor, incumbency will affect a candidate's general election campaign. The next section discusses this factor.

INCUMBENCY AND CAMPAIGNS

Incumbents are rightly believed to have great advantages over challengers. Part of the value of incumbency can be quantified: Congressmen seeking reelection in 1978, for example, were said to have a $547,191 advantage over their opponents.[5] However, the advantages extend far beyond the office staff, mailing privileges, and other quantifiable benefits that go with incumbency.

Incumbent Presidents, governors, mayors, and other executive officials often can establish the issues to be discussed in a campaign. An incumbent always has an advantage over his or her opponent in gaining free access to television and the newspapers. The air time given for presidential press conferences and addresses potentially can result in more positive impressions among viewers than can be obtained through purchased advertising, it is believed. This is particularly true in foreign affairs, where the President is seen as representing the nation. A trip abroad, a summit conference, a peace initiative can dominate the news—and perhaps stimulate a short-term "rally around the flag"[6] increase in public support for the President. Breakthroughs toward a Vietnam peace settlement were announced—prematurely in both cases—just prior to the 1968 and 1972 presidential elections.

Opposition candidates in some situations have to be cautious in criticizing executive office incumbents. A challenger would not want to seem to be undermining the President's negotiating position in foreign affairs, for example. A challenger would not want to base his or her campaign on an issue that the incumbent might be able to remove or confiscate by preelection action. The opposition can "only talk," while the incumbent can "do something about" issues raised by the opposition. An incumbent has a variety of choices: legislation can be signed or vetoed; administrative appointments can be made; funds can be released for water projects; commissions can be appointed; agencies can be reorganized; or the closing of a military base can be held up (at least until after the election). The incumbent can campaign yet not seem to be campaigning at all. A university that is happy to invite an incumbent President to speak on campus, even if he is campaigning for renomination or reelection, may be reluctant to do the same for an opposition party nominee. In 1976 Ford's so-called "Rose Garden campaign" called for him to spend as much time as possible, and as visibly as possible, being President. Nixon in 1972 and most previous Presidents also felt that they campaigned for reelection best by being seen to carry out the responsibilities of the office.

Thus, the usual experience of incumbents is that they are reelected. Of congressional incumbents who sought reelection in 1976, 93 percent were reelected. Many Congressional challengers are understandably pessimistic as to their prospects. Those who believe that they have "nothing to lose" by running will do so, which means that challengers often are persons lacking the resources necessary to win.[7] Since 1912 only two presidential incumbents have been defeated: Herbert Hoover in 1932, during the Depression; and Ford, the unelected incumbent in 1976. The four elections of Franklin D. Roosevelt (1932–1944) stimulated sufficient fear of the resources of the incumbent that the 22nd Amendment to the U.S. Constitution was ratified in 1951 to limit presidents to two terms. Several states (although a declining number) still limit governors to one term.

Some circumstances do favor nonincumbents. When there is division in the country, an opposition candidate might benefit from the freedom to remain ambiguous. This was true regarding the Vietnam War in 1968, when opposition candidate Richard Nixon promised an undefined "secret plan" to end the war. Incumbents sometimes face a coalition of minorities[8] unhappy about a number of different issues. At other times voters may feel that the need for new ideas is greater than the need for experience. Governors and mayors become vulnerable most frequently because of increased taxes, even though financial constraints may permit them few alternatives.[9]

Incumbency will have a still different meaning if it is combined with one-party dominance in a state. (See the box on "Tantamountcy.")

In the next section we will examine an increasingly important element of all campaigns, and particularly of presidential general election campaigns—the use of television.

TELEVISION

All enterprises are dependent upon some form of communication to inform members, staff, or supporters, but this is particularly true for political campaigns because they are not continuous activities. Campaigns arise from nowhere, must organize and fund themselves, and then prepare for a variety of activities in a short, frenetic period. A candidate with years of political experience, an established network of supporters, and seeking a low-visibility office, might not need the mass media. But most nominees for national or major statewide offices will depend on the mass media to tell potential workers, contributors, and voters that they exist, and why they exist.

Television is the omnipresent American communication medium. Despite hints in the ratings in the late 1970s that television viewing was declining among the middle-aged and young, television is expected to

Tantamountcy

In the solidly Democratic South of 1876–1948* it was often said that receiving the Democratic nomination was tantamount (equivalent) to election, and so
it was for almost all offices in almost all Southern states. Despite the spread of
competitive two-party politics in recent years, Democrats continue to hold most
state and local offices in the South, as Republicans do in several New England
and Plains states. In fact, at the state and local levels for most of the past century
close two-party competition has been more the exception in the nation than the
rule. The pattern of presidential elections conveys a distorted view of the
frequency of party alternation in office at most levels.

Clearly, general election campaigns will be quite different if the likelihood of
being defeated (or of winning, depending on one's perspective) is slim. In such
circumstances campaigns may involve lower costs and a shorter period of
intensive campaigning. The dominant party may direct its activities almost
entirely to getting out the vote rather than to activities designed to alter voter
choice. The minority party, with weak or nonexistent precinct organizations,
may rely more heavily on mass media advertising to reach voters—and hope
that a "coattail effect" from national candidates will benefit state and local
candidates.

*The classic study of Southern politics is V. O. Key, Jr., *Southern Politics in State
and Nation* (New York: Knopf, 1949).

continue to be the most effective (if not always the most efficient in cost
terms) way to reach large numbers of potential soap buyers or potential
voters. What is known about the possible impact of television on campaign outcomes?

First, political candidates demonstrate that they believe television
advertising is important because they spend great sums of money on it.
Either that or they do not want to take part in the experiment of not
spending money on television. Not knowing for certain what *does*
work, they do not want to risk omitting such a large item.

Presidential campaigns spend the largest part of their television bud-
gets in the month before election day, and usually the largest part of
that in the last week. Statewide campaigns commonly spend the largest
amount in the last 10 days before election day. The availability of public
funds in 1976 permitted both Presidential candidates to plan their
television usage in advance, and to hold to those schedules in most
instances. By contrast, the 1968 Humphrey campaign, severely
strapped for money, was forced to cancel two weeks of television spots

it had planned. Even so, it spent 61 percent of its $10.3 million budget on television.[10]

The second impact measure is audience size. Television has large audiences, permitting considerable exposure to messages, even if the results of such exposure are not certain.

Third, people identify television as their most important source of campaign information, although the meaning of such identification is unclear. National studies show that a reasonably stable two-thirds of respondents over the last quarter century have identified broadcast media as their most important source of campaign information. During this period there was a decline in the proportion identifying radio, and a corresponding increase in the proportion identifying television. Newspapers were identified as the most important source of information about campaigns by a stable one-quarter of respondents, with magazines being identified as most important by 5–8 percent.[11]

Fourth, there is fragmentary evidence, sometimes contradicted by other fragmentary evidence, that television news and political commercials do contribute to the public's knowledge of candidates and their positions.[12] The public knows about early election returns through television election night coverage. Whether this affects the voting behavior of West Coast voters has been the subject of considerable study. (See the box, "Early Returns.")

In the midst of uncertain claims about mass media impact, what is certain is that the development of television as the most widely used means of communication has affected how campaigns are conducted.

Early Returns

Are Californians who vote late in the afternoon (after the polls have closed on the East Coast, in a different time zone) affected by viewing returns from the East Coast? There might be a bandwagon effect, in which a candidate seen to be leading would receive more votes on the West Coast than he otherwise would have received. On the other hand, potential supporters of a candidate might be more likely to vote if they see he is trailing on the East Coast, or there might be a sympathy vote from the undecided for the trailing ("underdog") candidate. Although any of the above is plausible, studies to date suggest that viewing early returns has no important effect at all.*

*Kurt Lang and G. E. Lang, *Voting and Nonvoting* (Waltham, Mass.: Blaisdell, 1968); and Sam Tuchman and T. E. Coffin, "The Influence of Election Night Television Broadcasts in a Close Election," *Public Opinion Quarterly,* 35 (Fall 1971), pp. 315–326.

Television's impact on presidential general election campaigns has
been enormous, as we shall discuss below.

Checkers and Daisies

Just as radio presented Presidential candidates with a national audience for the first time in the 1920s and 1930s, television began in 1948
and more importantly in the 1950s to provide a national viewing audience for presidential candidates. Apart from the financing implications,
this new medium improved the prospects of candidates able to use it
effectively, and disadvantaged candidates whose appearance and
speaking styles were better suited to rallies on the courthouse steps.
"Could Abe Lincoln be elected now?" became the standard question.
A history of presidential campaigns since 1952 is, in part, a history of
the uses to which television has been put.

The major television event of 1952 was the "Checkers speech," a
national address by Richard Nixon delivered in an effort to prevent his
being removed as the vice presidential candidate on the Republican
ticket. Nixon had been accused of profiting personally from political
contributions. In an emotional (some would say maudlin) manner,
Nixon illustrated how television could be used to personalize political
issues. Nixon, his wife, and two daughters were in effect visiting other
families in their homes. Nixon bared his life and finances, and talked
about his wife's "respectable Republican cloth coat" and the black and
white cocker spaniel named Checkers he was determined to keep "regardless of what they say about it."[13] Nixon's closing appeal for support
was answered by thousands of letters and telegrams, and presidential
candidate Dwight Eisenhower decided to keep Nixon on the ticket.

Television spot commercials, 30- and 60-second advertisements designed to convey an image, were begun in the 1950s. If the purpose of
campaigns is to educate voters as to the issues and choices involved in
an election, are such commercials appropriate? Sixty seconds is too
short a period to do more than state a candidate's concern about a
problem or show a face and a name. There is time to suggest that the
candidate will do something about a problem, but rarely time to state
what the candidate will do. Of course, this ambiguity is one of the
attractions of television spots to candidates.

Some spots try to establish a mood by the settings in which the
candidates are placed. Adlai Stevenson (Democrat, 1952, 1956) was
shown leaning against a farm fence, and John Kennedy was shown
walking along the beach. The Kennedy spots stimulated a generation
of informal beach and coat-slung-over-the-shoulder footage. No restrictions have yet been imposed on political spots, and they have become
a staple of campaign advertising.

Spot commercials also may be used to dramatize the opposing candidate's alleged weaknesses. Perhaps the roughest presidential election, in terms of television attacks upon the opposition, was the 1964 Johnson–Goldwater race. The Democrats used a spot commercial showing a little girl picking the petals off a daisy, followed by pictures of a nuclear explosion and then reassuring statements by President Johnson. Like much of political advertising, this spot sought to exploit attitudes developed elsewhere—in this case fears about Senator Goldwater's position on use of nuclear weapons.[14] In 1976 the Ford campaign used brief shots of "average" Georgians criticizing home-state candidate Carter for his past performance as governor.

The 1960 election was marked by the first televised debates between presidential candidates. In the 1960s campaign organizations gave increasing attention to use of the uncontrolled media, that is, news and public affairs programs and print space. The carefully planned media event became a part of national and state campaigning.

In 1968 the managers of the Nixon campaign were faced with a serious media problem. They had a candidate who was well known to the voters, but whose image was not the most positive. Their candidate long had been at odds with the press—as exemplified by his self-characterized "final press conference" after his defeat in the California gubernatorial election of 1962. In that press conference he told the press it would not have Nixon "to kick around any more." His managers did not believe Nixon showed up well in the 1960 debates, and thus they intended to avoid any new debates. The producer of his 1968 television programs said:

> ... Let's face it, a lot of people think Nixon is dull. ... They look at him as the kind of kid who always carried a bookbag. Who was 42 years old the day he was born. They figure other kids get footballs for Christmas, Nixon got a briefcase and he loved it. He always had his homework done and he would never let you copy.
>
> Now you put him on television, you have got a problem right away. He is a funny looking guy. He looks like somebody hung him in a closet overnight and he jumps out in the morning with his suit all bunched up and starts running around saying, "I want to be President." I mean this is how he strikes some people. That is why these shows are important. To make them forget all that.[15]

The 1968 Nixon programs presented him almost entirely in controlled environments. In a series of staged events made to resemble press conferences people chosen by his organization would direct questions to Nixon, who would respond without benefit of notes or podium. These programs were designed to convey an image of an open and competent candidate, while protecting him from situations in which he might appear in an unfavorable light. It is not clear that this "selling of the President" was a success. Nixon's standing in the polls dropped steadily during that campaign, and he ultimately defeated Humphrey by only 1 percent of the vote.

Nixon's 1972 reelection campaign spent less than a third as much money as in 1968 on television and radio advertising and less than the McGovern campaign spent. Much of what the reelection campaign did spend was to show film clips of Nixon's trips abroad. The clips emphasized Nixon the President rather than Nixon the candidate. Also in 1972 a candidate seemingly tailor-made for television, the handsome mayor of New York City, John Lindsay, failed miserably in his media approach to the Democratic primaries. In the 1970s new approaches were developed to exploit the uncontrolled media. One was wider use of audio or video feeds, taped recordings of the candidate and other campaign spokesmen for free rebroadcast on news programs. The 1972 presidential campaigns were the only ones conducted under legal restrictions on the amount that could be spent on broadcasting. Yet campaign strategy rather than legal restrictions appeared to dictate Nixon's reduced investment in broadcasting in 1972. The 1976 campaigns were the first with public financing and the first since 1960 with presidential debates.

The Debates

Debates are not new in American politics. Debates on the courthouse steps were a familiar part of local and statewide campaigns in the past. The famed debates on slavery between Abraham Lincoln and Stephen Douglas were part of their contest for a U.S. Senate seat in Illinois. Instead of speaking to hundreds, however, television now offers far greater audiences.

In 1960 neither candidate was the presidential incumbent and neither held a wide lead in the polls. Nixon was the Vice President and well known, but he represented the minority party. John Kennedy was disadvantaged by his religious affiliation (Catholic) and by press concern about his experience and competence. Both felt they could benefit from appearing before the unprecedentedly large audiences that would view the debates: more than 75 million for the first debate, and approximately 50 million for each of the next three. Since neither the networks nor the major candidates wanted to provide time for the minor party candidates, Congress waived Section 315 of the Federal Communications Act requiring equal broadcast time to be given to all candidates for an office.

Answering the question "Who won the debates?" requires determination first of what it means to win. Winning is an artificial concept introduced by the news media, since the candidates presumably are not interested in winning the debates themselves, but rather in the contribution the debates can make to victory at the polls in November.[16] Thus, immediate surveys provide no evidence as to the true winners of debates.

The conventional wisdom is that Kennedy "won" the 1960 debates. Given the closeness of that election the debates and dozens of other factors with small impact could be identified as having been decisive, yet the debates apparently changed few votes.[17] Only after the first debate was there a sizable increase in poll standings for either candidate (for Kennedy in that case). What Kennedy may have won in that debate was an image of competency among those who were inclined to support him but were concerned about his relative inexperience. Kennedy may have impressed viewers with his command of statistics on a variety of problems. Or because he spoke to the camera (the audience), in contrast to Nixon who sometimes directed his comments to Kennedy as if to a debating opponent. Or because Nixon appeared pale and gaunt due to a short hospital stay, a too large collar, and a bad makeup job. Whether these factors influenced votes or not, they became part of the folklore surrounding the use of television.

Presidential debates were not held in 1964, 1968, and 1972 because in each case one candidate had a sufficiently large early lead that it did not appear to be in his interest to debate his opponent. (Debates were becoming more common in statewide races during this period.) In 1976 the incumbent President trailed in the polls, the Democratic challenger again needed to reassure supporters uncertain about his qualifications, and debates were agreed upon. Again Congress waived the equal time provision, and a series of presidential and vice presidential debates were conducted before television audiences of up to 70 million people.

What was the impact of these debates? When asked on election day by CBS-TV to choose as many as three reasons why they voted for Ford or Carter, only 10 percent of the sample identified the debates as an important reason. And 45 percent of that number also said they had made their voting decision prior to the debates. So the number who might have decided to vote for Ford or Carter because of the debates is fairly small. The CBS survey did not find that having watched the debates greatly affected the likelihood of voting.[18] Voting turnout overall was considerably lower than in the previous debate year. On the other hand, opinion poll rankings of candidates before and after the debates have been used to argue that the second debate was decisive in halting Carter's decline. His poll lead had dwindled from 16–17 percent in early September to 2–4 percent by early October, but after the second debate the decline halted.[19] That debate related to foreign policy, an area in which Carter was seen as inexperienced. Yet it was

Ford in that debate who made the error of asserting that Eastern European countries were not dominated by the Soviet Union.

Whether debates will be worth the candidate's time and effort in the future—Ford and Carter virtually ceased their campaigns for several days before each debate—depends on the context in which they occur. Debates may prove more attractive to candidates for statewide office lacking access to public funds. In campaigns in which experience and expertise appear to be the most valued qualities, candidates able to demonstrate these qualities on television may profit from debates. Other qualities, such as honesty, are not easily demonstrated on television. Debates give a candidate access to some of his or her opponent's supporters, in a neutral and authoritative format, and for this reason debates always will have the potential to affect campaigns and voter choices.

In this and previous chapters we have discussed many of the choices facing parties, candidates, and campaign managers. Now we come to the day on which voters must make their choices.

ON ELECTION DAY

The campaign planning, the targeting of voting groups as potential supporters, the door-knocking and broadcasting, all of this is directed to influencing the behavior of potential voters on election day. Whether it is a party primary or a general election, the goals of a campaign remain the same: reinforce and activate your supporters and, where possible, convert your opponents.

Election week activities are designed to protect the gains of previous months. During the several days prior to an election a candidate's potential supporters have been reminded to vote, and have been offered assistance in getting to the polls. Radio advertising may be used on election day to reach voters at home, at work, and in the car—to reach those who have not yet voted, and perhaps to activate a few who might not otherwise vote. Poll-watchers are utilized to guard against improper activities by opposing candidates, who have poll-watchers of their own, of course. Election days in the United States in recent years have been more circumspect than the one described by novelist Charles Dickens in mid-nineteenth century England (see box on "Election Day Roundup–Dickens Style"). For one thing, many states now close the bars and liquor stores on election day.

Some endorsements come in late. Newspapers usually wait until the last two weeks before election day to endorse candidates editorially, and some wait until the last day or two. In a few cases local interest groups wait until the night before the election to announce their endorsements.

Election Day Roundup – Dickens Style

Charles Dickens, a century and a quarter ago, described a spirited English election day. Prospective voters were kept in brandy and beer. Campaign managers sought to lock up their voters on election eve, lest the opposition get to them, while bribing barmaids to drug the brandy of opposing voters and inducing coachmen to tip their carriages full of opposition voters into the canal. Much kissing of babies occurred, and there were green parasols as gifts for the ladies.

> During the whole time of the polling, the town was in a perpetual fever of excitement. Everything was conducted on the most liberal and delightful scale. [Beverages] were remarkably cheap at all the public-houses, and . . . vans paraded the streets for the accommodation of voters who were seized with any temporary dizziness in the head—an epidemic which prevailed among the electors . . . to a most alarming extent, and under the influence of which they might frequently be seen lying on the pavements in a state of utter insensibility. A small body of electors remained unpolled on the very last day. They were calculating and reflecting persons, who had not yet been convinced by the arguments of either party, although they had frequent conferences with each. One hour before the close of the poll, Mr. Perker [campaign manager for Mr. Slumkey] solicited the honour of a private interview with these intelligent, these noble, these patriotic men. It was granted. His arguments were brief, but satisfactory. They went in a body to the poll and when they returned, the honourable Samuel Slumkey, of Slumkey Hall, was returned also.*

Pickwick Papers (New York: Modern Library, n.d.), p. 179. (Parenthetical phrases added.)

The act of voting involves pulling a lever on a machine or marking a ballot with a hole-puncher or pencil. In most, but not all, places balloting is done in a booth to insure secrecy of the ballot. The form and arrangement of the ballot may be of importance. In the 1948 presidential election there was a dispute in several Southern states as to whether the national Democratic candidate (Harry Truman) or the States Rights candidate (Strom Thurmond) would be given the ballot place of the Democratic party. Location within the list of candidates for an office is believed to be important in low-visibility races with a large number of candidates.[20] In states with a long ballot, bottom-of-the-ticket races may be skipped over entirely by many voters.

Candidates are concerned, strictly speaking, with winning elections, not winning votes. Votes must be combined or aggregated according to some system for a candidate to be declared the winner. In the next section we will discuss several systems of vote aggregation.

SYSTEMS OF VOTE AGGREGATION

Voting occurs within prescribed geographical areas. States and localities have a variety of choices as to how constituencies will be defined, what their geographic scope will be, and the number of candidates who will compete within them. City council members might be elected on partisan or nonpartisan ballots. Council members and state legislators might be elected in single-member districts in which they must reside (a city ward or district system), or all candidates in a jurisdiction could compete against one another, with the top vote-getters across the entire area declared the winners (an at-large system). A plurality usually is sufficient to win the general election. This is true of congressional and statewide offices. (For elections without candidates, see the box, "Elections in Which No One Is Elected.")

The electoral mechanism by which Presidents are chosen is distinctive, and requires a separate discussion.

The Electoral College

Each state has electoral votes equal to the number of its U.S. senators (two) and U.S. representatives (based on population). A presidential candidate could win a plurality or even a majority of the popular votes in the general election, yet lose the office because he failed to win a majority of the electoral votes of the states. This is not a hypothetical contingency. In 1824, 1876, and 1888 the leader in popular votes lost the election because he trailed in electoral votes. Current concern grows out of the close elections of 1960, 1968, and 1976, in which small changes in popular votes could have altered the Electoral College outcome.

In 1960 Kennedy won only 118,000 more popular votes than Nixon. Kennedy carried Illinois by less than 9,000 out of 4.75 million votes cast, but because of the winner-take-all plurality principle that operates in the award of electoral votes, Kennedy received all of its electoral votes. In 1968 Humphrey trailed Nixon by only 510,000 popular votes, but lost by a 301–191 margin in the Electoral College. Third party candidate George Wallace, hoping to win enough electoral votes to prevent either Humphrey or Nixon from winning a majority in the Electoral College, won only 46 electoral votes. If he had won enough to deny a majority to anyone, Wallace indicated he might exchange his support for policy or appointment concessions from one of the major party candidates. If

Elections in Which No One Is Elected

Most elections are designed to choose executive, legislative, or judicial office-holders from among the available candidates—that is, to choose from among people rather than programs or laws. As alternatives to representative decision-making, the Populist and Progressive movements of the 1890s–1910s put forward several techniques of direct democracy. These include: (a) the initiative, the prerogative of a portion of the electorate to place a legislative proposal on the ballot for direct vote by the electorate; (b) the referendum, in which voters review laws passed by the legislature; and (c) the recall, in which a portion of the electorate may force (prior to normal election dates) a vote on whether specified office-holders may continue in their offices.

Local property tax or school assessment votes have long been common, as have referenda on bond issues. Popular votes on constitutional amendments are a long tradition. Now the Populist-Progressive forms of direct democracy, used relatively rarely until the past decade, are increasingly utilized. Twenty-three states and hundreds of cities permit the initiative in various forms, and proposition voting has become particularly prevalent in California. An example is Proposition 13, a successful 1978 measure in California to cut property taxes. In the late 1970s some support existed to amend the U.S. Constitution to permit the initiative for national legislation. Thirty-eight states permit referenda, again in various forms. The recall is almost universal in state law, but rarely used.*
If initiative and referendum voting become common, new descriptions may be necessary as to how voters are likely to behave and how campaigns are likely to be organized.

*Les Ledbetter, "More and More, Voters Write Law," *The New York Times,* October 30, 1977, pp. 1, 22.

no candidate had won a majority of electoral votes in 1968, and assuming that no electors defied tradition and cast their votes for someone other than the winner in their states, the selection of the President would have been left to the U.S. House of Representatives. In the House Congressmen would vote by states with each state then having one vote for President.

In 1976 Ford trailed Carter by 1,681,000 votes out of 80 million votes cast, but it was only 11,116 votes in Ohio and 35,245 votes in Wisconsin that kept him from retaining the Presidency. Winning those two states would have given Ford an Electoral College majority. In each of these recent elections, the plurality winner in popular votes also has won a majority of electoral votes, but the margins have been so close as to encourage proposals to change the system.

One problem, then, is that the Electoral College does not *necessarily* reflect the wishes of a national plurality of the voters. The remedy proposed is usually direct election of the President, with abolition of the Electoral College. Another complaint is that electoral votes overrepresent certain kinds of states. Since Senators are allocated equally to all states regardless of population, there is a slight bias in favor of smaller population states. However, this bias is more than compensated for by the weight that the winner-take-all provision gives to larger population states (that tend also to be urban and industrial states). A narrow popular vote victory in California gives the candidate all of that state's electoral votes. It is worth more than overwhelming victories in half a dozen small-population states. Time spent by a candidate in less populated states (for example, Nixon's 1960 visit to Alaska, as part of his 50-state tour) reduces the time that can be spent in an important state (for example, Illinois, lost by Nixon by a narrow margin in 1960). Every presidential campaign (except Goldwater's in 1964) plans to carry a significant number of the larger population states and this disproportionate campaign attention presumably influences the kinds of candidates nominated and the kinds of issues with which candidates identify themselves. Democrats Kennedy and Carter aimed for the large industrial states plus the South, for example, and most Republican candidates aim for the same industrial states (perhaps excluding Massachusetts and New Jersey) plus the smaller Plains and Western states.

Defenders of the Electoral College say that problems could be solved short of dismantling the system. The possibility that electors would cast ballots for a candidate other than the one who led in their state could be removed while leaving the system of voting by states. Having electoral votes cast by states, it is argued, prevents further weakening of the party system and further movement toward mass media-dominated campaigns. The present system recognizes the political heterogeneity of the country and forces campaign organizations to deal with this heterogeneity. The Electoral College bias in favor of urban, industrial states, it is argued, has in the past compensated for a small-town and rural bias in Congress. Efforts in the late 1970s to persuade Congress to pass on to the states a constitutional amendment abolishing the Electoral College were not initially successful.

We will conclude this chapter with a brief summary.

WHY IT IS A MINOR MIRACLE THAT ANYONE IS ELECTED

Taken literally, of course, the above heading is inaccurate because, assuming there is at least one candidate, someone has to be elected to each office. But it is something of a minor miracle when political campaigns achieve any of their intermediate goals—turnout, conversion, and so forth. In looking at campaign organizations one must forget stereotypes of well-oiled machinery, legions of disciplined and enthusiastic supporters, and acres of money. Occasionally, a presidential or gubernatorial campaign might approximate the ideal. More typically, campaign organizations can be described as intermittently structured chaos. Too few people with too little experience try to achieve too much in too little time with too little money. So it is remarkable when they accomplish anything at all.

The extent to which campaigns are worthwhile depends on how strictly the word "campaign" is defined. In most presidential nomination campaigns since 1936 the leaders at the outset of the active campaign period have been the ultimate nominees.[21] However, differentiating between campaign and precampaign periods is becoming increasingly difficult. Candidates often begin running for an office several years before the election. Thus, the candidate standings at the beginning of an election year may have been influenced already by campaign activities.

Only a small minority of the electorate will make late voting decisions and may be influenced by late campaign activities, but in close elections that minority may account for the margin of victory or defeat. True conversion may occur only in a few cases, but these may be a critical few. Although vote change often receives more attention, reinforcement and activation occur more frequently. The outcome of many elections is determined by the success of campaign organizations in getting their supporters to the polls. This is especially true for Democrats.

Thus, campaigns do matter. In the final chapter we will evaluate alternative views of where American electoral politics is headed.

FOR FURTHER READING

Many studies of nomination campaigns cited in Chapter 6 also deal with general election campaigns. Campaigning by challengers is dealt with in Jeff Fishel, *Party and Opposition: Congressional Challengers in American Politics* (New York: McKay, 1973). Also see John W. Kingdon, *Candidates for Office* (New York: Random House, 1966). Third party campaigns are discussed by Mazmanian.[22] A substantial literature exists on the question of how peoples' voting preferences can best be aggregated. This somewhat arcane literature is relevant to party convention and Electoral College reform proposals. See, for example, James Buchanan and Gordon Tullock, *The Calculus of Consent* (Ann Arbor: University of Michigan Press, 1962). On the mathematical difficulties of deciding between more than two possibilities, see Kenneth Arrow, *Social Choice and Individual Values* (New York: Wiley, 1963).

NOTES

1. On the Wallace campaign see Daniel A. Mazmanian, *Third Parties in Presidential Elections* (Washington: Brookings Institution, 1974).

2. Hubert Humphrey in 1968 (before public financing) was an exception. See the brief discussion below.

3. On psychologically inaccessible information, see Robert L. Kahn and Charles F. Cannell, *The Dynamics of Interviewing* (New York: Wiley, 1957), pp. 151 ff.

4. Robert Agranoff, *The Management of Election Campaigns* (Boston: Holbrook, 1976), p. 76; and Robert G. Lehnen, "Stability of Presidential Choice in 1968: The Case of Two Southern States," *Social Science Quarterly,* 51 (June 1970), pp. 138–147.

5. "Incumbents' Funds Advantage On Rise," *Greensboro Daily News,* November 14, 1977.

6. This concept is discussed in John E. Mueller, "Presidential Popularity from Truman to Johnson," *American Political Science Review,* 64 (March 1970), pp. 18–34.

7. Linda L. Fowler, "The Electoral Lottery: Decisions to Run for Congress" (Paper delivered at the American Political Science Association annual meeting, Chicago, September 1976).

8. This concept also is discussed in Mueller, "Presidential Popularity . . . "

9. See James Clotfelter and William R. Hamilton, "Electing a Governor in the Seventies," in Thad Beyle and J. Oliver Williams, Eds., *The American Governor in Behavioral Perspective* (New York: Harper, 1972).

10. Herbert E. Alexander, *Political Financing* (Minneapolis: Burgess, 1972), p. 10.

11. Herbert Asher, *Presidential Elections and American Politics* (Homewood, Ill.: Dorsey, 1976), p. 223.

12. For example, see Robert D. McClure and Thomas E. Patterson, "Television News and Voter Behavior in the 1972 Presidential Election" (Paper delivered at the American Political Science Association annual meeting, New Orleans, September 1973). Also see the discussion in Chapter 5 of the 1940s and more recent studies of the impact of the communication media on vote choice.

13. Marvin R. Weisbord, *Campaigning for President* (New York: Washington Square Press, 1966), p. 182.

14. The Goldwater campaign produced, but did not use, a television program every bit as rough as the daisy spot. Interspersed between shots of topless dancing, crime in the streets, and other social phenomena presumably attributable to the Democrats, were shots of an unidentified limousine careening over the prairies with beer cans flying out the driver's window. A short time earlier President Johnson had taken newsmen for a celebrated tour of his Texas ranch—complete with allegedly reckless driving and beer drinking.

15. Joe McGinniss, *The Selling of the President, 1968* (New York: Trident, 1969), p. 103.

16. Warren J. Mitofsky, "1976 Presidential Debate Effects: A Hit or a Myth" (Paper presented at the American Political Science Association annual meeting, Washington, September 1977), pp. 1–2.

17. Elihu Katz and Jacob J. Feldman, "The Debates in the Light of Research: A Survey of Surveys," in Sidney Kraus, Ed., *The Great Debates* (Bloomington: Indiana University, 1962), pp. 173–223.

18. Mitofsky, "1976 Presidential Debate Effects . . . ," pp. 3–5.

19. Burns W. Roper, "The Effects of the Debates on the Carter/Ford Election," pp. 1–6; also see Paul H. Hagner and John Orman, "A Panel Study of the Impact of the First 1976 Presidential Debate" (both presented at the American Political Science Association annual meeting, Washington, September 1977).

20. Gary C. Byrne and J. Kristian Pueschel, "But Who Should I Vote for for County Coroner?" *Journal of Politics,* 37 (August 1974), pp. 778–784.

21. See Chapter 6. Also see William R. Keech and Donald R. Matthews, *The Party's Choice* (Washington: Brookings Institution, 1976), Chapters 3–4.

22. *Third Parties in Presidential Elections* (Washington: Brookings Institution, 1974).

CHAPTER 8

Trends in American Politics

In the preceding chapters we have described and analyzed various aspects of elections. Our examination of the dimensions of the electoral process has involved several perspectives. We have discussed both the behavior of voters and the behavior of candidates and other campaign participants, and we have covered the process of candidate recruitment and nomination as well as behavior in the general election. Having discussed the components of the electoral process, we now will look at the system as a whole, summarizing recent trends and considering future directions.

PARTIES, ELECTIONS, AND THE CRISIS OF CONFIDENCE

In one important way the system of elections is in trouble: it fails to enjoy the confidence of the American people. Survey data from the 1960s and 1970s show a dramatic decline in public confidence in elections and parties, to the point where negative attitudes now prevail. In 1976, for example, respondents in a national survey were asked which national political institution—President, Congress, Supreme Court, or political parties—they least trusted to do the right thing. The overwhelming majority, 70 percent, singled out parties as the institution they least trusted.[1] In the same survey, 64 percent of the respondents agreed that political parties were interested only in people's votes, not in their opinions.[2] Data from other opinion polls confirm what these results suggest: people have limited faith in the electoral process, and cynicism, suspicion, and distrust characterize the reaction of many to elections, candidates, and parties.

The growth of negative attitudes toward the electoral process is part of a broader decline in the confidence that the American people have in their political institutions. As mentioned in Chapter 1, the 1960s and 1970s were a period of growing political alienation, which was manifested in public reactions along several dimensions. In general, people now express far less confidence in their government, less trust in their political leaders, and less faith in the political process. These negative attitudes began to spread in the mid-1960s and continued to grow through the mid-1970s.[3] Recent public opinion data indicate that the decline in political confidence and trust has been arrested but not reversed, and political alienation currently stands at a high level.

This increased alienation seems to be largely a result of the events of the 1960s and 1970s. The Vietnam War deeply divided the population and produced intense dissatisfaction from both the left and the right with government policy. The urban riots and domestic unrest of the late 1960s, exemplified by the violent demonstrations surrounding the 1968 Democratic National Convention, also contributed to a growing lack of confidence in the system. Coming when it did, Watergate did more than just discredit the Nixon administration and embarrass the Republican Party; it reinforced and fostered the already growing feeling that political leaders were not to be trusted. Although there have not been such divisive issues or events in the late 1970s, the inability of both parties to deal with the problems of inflation, unemployment, and energy shortages has done little to improve public confidence in American political institutions and processes.

Paralleling this increased alienation is a decline in electoral participation. As mentioned earlier in this book, turnout in American elections has been falling since the early 1960s. This drop has occurred despite several developments that should have increased turnout: (a) the legal mechanisms used to keep blacks from voting in the South have been eliminated, and blacks have begun to vote in significant numbers in that region; (b) educational levels among the adult population have risen, which should have increased turnout because more highly educated individuals are more likely to vote; and (c) residency requirements have been reduced sharply, and they no longer disenfranchise as many individuals. In light of these developments the drop-off in turnout is all the more significant.

Americans not only feel more negatively toward the electoral process; they also are participating in it less. Of course, we cannot equate nonvoting with political alienation. There are people who hold cynical, suspicious, and distrustful views of the government and still go to the polls. Conversely, some of those who do not vote are not politically alienated, but are simply passive and apathetic. The increases in non-voting, however, parallel the attitude changes discussed above for obvious reasons. As people have become more negative in their reaction to the electoral process, they have less motivation to participate in it. Lower turnout rates, like the results of recent public opinion polls, are a reflection of the general political malaise that has settled on this country.

Declining turnout has resulted in voters being less representative of the population. Because not all vote, and because those who do vote differ in predictable ways from those who do not, voters always have been unrepresentative of the entire adult population, as we pointed out in Chapter 2. The recent increases in nonvoting have merely widened an existing gap.[4] From our earlier discussions we know which groups will be the most underrepresented among the ranks of the voters: the poor, the uneducated, and the underprivileged—precisely those groups that have few ways of being heard except through the ballot box.

The unrepresentative nature of voters is probably greatest in low-turnout elections, such as most local elections and primary elections at all levels. Even presidential primaries may be quite unrepresentative. The fight between Ford and Reagan for the 1976 Republican presidential nomination illustrates this. Ford and Reagan divided the primary vote fairly evenly, despite the fact that public opinion polls showed Ford to be far more popular among Republicans.[5] Those who actually voted in the Republican presidential primaries were far from a representative cross section of all Republicans. The success of the Reagan forces in the presidential primaries shows that low-turnout elections provide an opportunity for a group to exercise disproportionate influence by getting a high proportion of its followers to the polls. None of this is likely to increase public confidence in the electoral process. Instead, the decisions reached by a small and unrepresentative set of voters will, more likely, reinforce the existing high levels of cynicism, suspicion, and distrust that exist among the general public.

Concern over the low turnout in American elections has been expressed by many political leaders. President Carter proposed a system of election day registration for federal elections. Vice President Mondale, speaking for the proposal, cited his home state as an example of what legal changes might accomplish: ". . . Minnesota, which has used Election Day registration since 1974, had a turnout in the last election of nearly 72 percent, the highest in the nation."[6] Reforming registration procedures would have some impact, and other legal reforms (such as multilingual ballots in appropriate areas) also might help. However desirable, legal changes can only do so much. An optimistic estimate of the total impact of the various legal reforms that have been proposed is that turnout in presidential elections would be increased by 10 to 12 percentage points.[7] The impact for nonpresidential elections would be less. Larger increases in electoral participation will require changes in people's feelings about the electoral process as well as changes in rules and regulations.

Renewed confidence in the electoral process could result from changes in the political party system. An altered party system might encourage greater interest in elections, greater concern over election outcomes, stronger feelings of political efficacy, and greater satisfaction with the electoral process. In particular, two aspects of the current party system may be identified as contributing to the negative attitudes that are so commonly held toward the electoral process: the lack of two-party competition below the presidential level and the weakness of existing party organizations. A party system marked by greater competition between stronger and more cohesive parties might help to renew public confidence in the electoral process.

THE DECOMPOSITION OF AMERICAN POLITICAL PARTIES

Throughout this book we have described how parties have come to play a weaker role in the electoral process. The main aspect of this can be briefly summarized: voters are less attached to parties and less guided in their voting by any notion of party loyalty; candidates are increasingly forming their own campaign organizations and running their campaigns without reliance on party organizations; and party organizations are exercising less influence over nominations, with the most notable change occurring at the presidential level. The cumulative effect of this is what some commentators term a decomposition of the party system.[8] The reasons for this party decomposition also have been discussed in previous chapters: changes in media-use patterns; development of new campaign methods; reforms designed to open up or democratize parties and elections; changes in campaign finance laws and practices; and the growth of a more educated and sophisticated electorate. Having discussed how and why parties have become a less relevant part of the electoral process, we now consider what the impact of this change is.

What useful purposes do political parties play in elections? They serve to structure the vote, simplify choices for the voter, and make elections more meaningful. If we did not have parties, most voters would find elections chaotic and confusing. As one analyst states:

> There are so many different elective offices in a country like the U.S. that citizens cannot consider their votes meaningful instruments for policy control unless the myriad separate contests are linked up in some under-

standable fashion—unless, for instance, balloting for the 435 seats of a legislature can be seen as a struggle of one party against another, rather than unrelated, detached vying of individuals.[9]

One way in which parties serve to structure electoral competition is by indicating the basic party commitments of the candidates. In this sense, the party label serves as a guide to the voter. Lacking specific information about the candidate in a particular race, the voter can use the party label as a cue to what the candidate probably stands for. For the highly visible offices—president, governor, senator, for example— this may not be so important, as most voters may be capable of acquiring sufficient information about the candidates. But for the less visible offices most voters cannot or will not learn enough about what the candidates stand for to be able to make a meaningful choice without the help of a party label. This is probably true even for a major office such as U.S. representative. When voters do not find party labels useful, either because they see no differences between the parties or because they do not care about the things that the parties differ over, the result is likely to be a more confused and alienated electorate.

Another way in which parties serve to structure electoral competition is by providing a clear basis for reward and punishment. Elections are mechanisms through which voters can reward those in power for governing well or punish those in power for doing poorly. As one political analyst points out:

> One common type of political rhetoric is that which points out unsolved problems and condemns the failures of opponents. It is most enthusiastic and effective when times are bad, due to war, depression, or civil unrest; the voters are discontented, and a challenger attacks the performance of the incumbent president and his party. In such cases, in fact, the reality of bad times speaks largely for itself, and the job of the challenger is simply to draw attention to it, to fasten the blame securely on the incumbents, and to promise that things will be better under his administration.[10]

For electoral behavior to reflect these considerations in a meaningful way, parties must structure the competition between the ins and the outs. Parties must be the recipients of the rewards and punishments. For example, if a voter is dissatisfied with the performance of his state legislature, it may be too much to ask that he determine the particular legislators responsible for the poor performance and vote on that basis in the next election. The voter almost certainly will lack the information necessary for that task, and he may even be faced with a choice between nonincumbents in the next legislative election. The most feasible way for the voter to operate is to punish the party in power and reward the opposition party. If voters react in this fashion, it will create pressure on the parties to perform well when in power:

> ... it would make sense for the public to judge performance on a party basis. Even if Adlai Stevenson in 1952 had nothing whatever to do with corruption in Washington, or the war in Korea, or the "loss" of China, it was appropriate to punish him and other Democratic candidates in order to create incentives for all members of the governing party—whether in or out of national office—to put pressure on their fellow partisans to make things work. Similarly, it was reasonable to hold Humphrey accountable for Johnson's performance in 1968, and Ford for Nixon's in 1976.[11]

The decomposition of the party system makes it less likely that voters will feel that voting for the opposition party is a meaningful way of expressing dissatisfaction with the way they are being governed. Instead, dissatisfaction may be translated into a general reaction against all incumbents. There are signs that this type of behavior is on the increase. Several candidates in the 1976 presidential primaries—Carter, Reagan, and Brown, for example—were able to achieve success by projecting images of outsiders untainted by the mess in Washington. Even after he had been president for almost three years, President Carter in late 1979 was seeking to picture himself as an anti-Washington figure. The same phenomenon has occurred at other levels as well. As one analyst states, " . . . increasingly, the road to victory lies in a candidate's successfully denying that he ever had anything to do with politics before."[12]

Political parties also can serve to aggregate diverse interests. In this sense, parties are coalition builders that blend together diverse particular interests. The demise of parties has meant the loss of this interest aggregation, with the result that interest groups have become more influential in the electoral process. One way that interest groups can exercise influence is by attempting to mobilize their supporters to work and vote for or against a particular candidate. Another way in which such groups exercise influence is through campaign contributions. The campaign reforms of the 1970s permit groups and organizations to form political action committees (PACs), through which campaign contributions can be channelled to individual candidates. The importance of political action committees has increased in recent years. In 1974, several hundred PACs contributed about $12 million to congressional candidates; in 1976 over one thousand PACs channelled over $22 million to congressional candidates; and in 1978 close to two thousand PACs gave an estimated $35 million to congressional candidates.[13]

Especially interesting are groups that are concerned with a single and relatively narrow issue, such as gun control, abortion, the Equal Rights

Amendment, nuclear power, or consumer protection. Such groups are often intensely committed to a certain position and intolerant toward office holders who do not fully support the group's position. These groups seem to have become more significant in recent years. Add to these the many business, labor, and other economic interest groups, and one can understand why many candidates complain about being opposed by a group because of a vote on a single bill. The decomposition of the party system has left candidates less insulated from the demands of highly particularized interest groups. This view is succinctly expressed by one scholar:

> ... political parties, with all their well-known human and structural shortcomings, are the only devices thus far invented by the wit of Western man which with some effectiveness can generate countervailing collective power on behalf of the many individually powerless against the relatively few who are individually—or organizationally—powerful.[14]

American parties always have been fairly weak organizations, at least in comparison to the highly centralized and cohesive party organizations found in many European democracies. Current developments have made our parties even weaker, perhaps at a time when stronger party organizations were needed. Reversing this trend may not be easy. Some changes, such as altering campaign finance laws and practices to channel more money through the parties, would strengthen the party organizations. However, some legal and structural changes that would have a significant impact probably would not draw much support. It does not seem likely, for example, that the trends in presidential nominating practices will be reversed and the situation returned to that of earlier periods. Furthermore, many of the sources of party decomposition—new campaign methods, the increased importance of television, the greater independence of voters—cannot be legislated away.

THE LACK OF PARTY COMPETITION

The present party system is not marked by vigorous two-party competition. Decomposition of the party system has not altered the overall party balance. The Democrats remain the majority party in the country. Both houses of Congress remained safely in the hands of the Democrats throughout the 1960s and 1970s. Control of state government has also been marked by Democratic domination. Only 18 of the 50 governors are Republicans, and in only 12 states does the Republican Party have a majority in both houses of the state legislature. In fact, the Republicans have declined in strength over the past two decades to the point that some observers feel they have become a permanent minority party.

Even as Republican fortunes at lower levels were ebbing in the 1970s, the party remained competitive in presidential elections. Except for the 1964 debacle, Republican presidential candidates won or nearly won every presidential election from 1948 on. The result is a "two-tiered" party system. At the presidential level neither party dominates, the situation is unstable, and outcomes are unpredictable. Below the presidential level, the Democrats dominate, the situation is more stable, and outcomes are more predictable. Republicans will continue to be strong contenders for the presidency, but whether they will be able to take over other levels and branches of government is far less certain.

The growing separation of presidential and congressional voting is one example of these tendencies. Competitive congressional seats are those that can be won by either party in any given election. In the past the election outcome in these marginal districts in presidential election years often depended on how the presidential vote went in the district. If one presidential candidate did much better in the district, his "coattails" usually would help the congressional candidate of his party to victory. Lyndon Johnson's defeat of Barry Goldwater in 1964 was not merely a defeat of the Republican presidential candidate; Johnson's coattails carried numerous Democratic congressional candidates to Washington. But in 1972, Nixon's landslide victory lacked the same coattail effect, and the Democrats retained clear control of Congress. The coattail effect has diminished and the number of marginal seats has shrunk.[15] Increasingly, congressional candidates have become less affected by the outcome of the presidential election. Only a small minority of the congressmen elected in any year will have faced a grueling challenge in the general election, and once elected, congressmen usually can count on being returned to office.

The elimination of a close relationship between presidential voting and congressional voting reflects the growth of ticket-splitting. The increased tendency of voters to divide their ballots goes beyond the top of the ticket, however. It is equally prevalent in state and local elections. This ticket-splitting, in turn, reflects a greater candidate orientation in American elections. The effect of this is to magnify the benefits of incumbency, at least for the less-visible offices. For many offices, most voters have such limited information about the candidates that they are forced to cast their ballot on the basis of party labels and general familiarity with the candidates. As the party label exercises less influence on voting, simple name recognition becomes more important in the balloting for the less visible offices, and here incumbents have a great advantage over challengers. Americans may pride themselves on the fact that they vote for the person, not the party. Unfortunately, this has resulted in congressional elections in which incumbents are rarely defeated, as we have mentioned above. Different patterns exist for the most visible offices, however. There the behavior of the electorate is more volatile and unpredictable. Some examples of this are the difficulty that President Ford had in the presidential primaries in 1976 and the inability of such well-known senators as Edward Brooke and Clifford Case to win reelection in 1978.

If anything, party competition has lessened over the past two decades. We now have what some observers term a "one-and-a-half" party system. The absence of regular two-party competition for many offices in many areas means that voters often lack the opportunity of choosing between a structured set of alternatives. Many voters may find that a vehicle through which they can express dissatisfaction is lacking. Certainly this does little to build public confidence in the electoral process.

To sum up our discussion thus far, political parties can be instruments for popular control of government. In a nation of over 200 million people, we need political institutions to act as mediators or transmission belts between governing elites and the people. Parties can fill this role, and strong and competitive parties can do it much better than weak and uncompetitive parties.

TOWARD A NEW PARTY SYSTEM

To many analysts, the developments we have described show that the existing party system is no longer relevant to the contemporary social and political situation. They see the current party system as a product of an earlier industrial period and the decomposition of that system as a natural result of its growing irrelevance. If this view is correct, then strong and competitive political parties are likely to be created only through a critical realignment.

We have discussed the general nature of realignment in earlier chapters. In several ways, a critical realignment might alter or reverse the trends we have discussed in this chapter. First, a realignment could produce more cohesive parties by providing each party with a more salient reason for existence. Second, party labels might become more meaningful to voters, as they would more easily find differences between the policy orientations of the parties (as happened in the 1930s). Third, voter interest and enthusiasm might be stimulated by a new party system, leading to increased turnout. Fourth, a realignment could serve to create a more competitive party system, although this is by no means a necessary result of realignment.

Could a realignment occur? The answer to this question surely must be "Yes," given our discussions of the decomposition of political parties and the breakup of the New Deal coalition. What would cause a realignment and what would the outcome be? This is a more difficult question to answer. Economic and regional divisions are most likely to be involved in a realignment, and we may examine these two factors.

Class divisions appear to be declining in American politics, as we have discussed earlier. The affluence of the past 30 years has transformed much of the working class from have-nots to haves. Most working-class families, families where the head of the household is a blue-collar worker, are well above the subsistence level. It is now fairly commonplace to see working-class families living in ranch homes with color television, owning two cars and perhaps a camping trailer, and sending their children to college. This is not to say that economic inequalities no longer exist and that poverty has been eliminated. It is true, however, that much of the white working class can consider itself economically established, and this has implications for their political behavior. The disproportionate support that the Northern, white, ethnic working class provided to the New Deal Democratic coalition was based in part on their support of interventionist economic and welfare policies. The blue-collar labor force no longer can be counted on to be so supportive of income redistribution and social welfare programs; many now see such policies as benefiting not them but those below them. Also, ethnic and religious cleavages are less significant today, because they were in large part based on their relationship to class differences.

Class voting has declined also because of changes in the occupational and economic structure. The movement toward a postindustrial economy has blurred the difference between white-collar and blue-collar workers and has introduced new economic issues into the political arena. The result is that many significant questions of economic policy are not class-related. The newer economic issues concern, among other things, inflation, pollution, energy, and consumer protection. Support for government intervention on some of these issues tends to be more widespread among the better-off groups. College-educated professionals, for example, are more supportive of strict government regulation in the areas of pollution control, and natural resource protection than are blue-collar workers.[16] Other economic issues tend to cut across occupational lines. Inflation, for example, appears to be a concern of everyone. Many of these new economic issues are likely to remain important in the 1980s, and there is little reason to believe that attitudes on these issues will be any more related to occupational or economic position than they are now. Economic issues and conflict are therefore likely to be a part of American politics in the future, but class conflict will be relatively absent.

Perhaps the movement toward a postindustrial economy will produce new economic cleavages. Significant changes in the occupational structure, including expansion of the service sector and the knowledge industries, are part of the development of a postindustrial economy. We can only speculate on what political cleavages might emerge in the future; two possibilities can be noted.

One cleavage that may take on increased significance in the future is between the public and private sectors. Expansion of the government generally is seen as part of the development of a postindustrial economy, but recent events suggest that conflict over the extent and financing of the public sector will be important in the 1980s. Those employed by government—federal, state, or local—share some common concerns and goals. They are vulnerable to two threats: inflation and taxpayer revolts. Increased productivity may not be possible in many areas of the public sphere, distinguishing it from the industrial sector. Increased wages and salaries for government employees must be financed out of increased taxes. Attempts to both increase the size of the public sector and provide cost-of-living increases to public employees imply significantly higher taxes in an era of high inflation rates. Many of those in the private sector prefer lower taxes to increased government services and higher pay scales for public employees. Conflict over the size of the government budget and the rate of taxation undoubtedly will be present in the 1980s, as it has been in past decades. What may be new is a greater intensity to this split and a relatively permanent occupational cleavage along these lines.

Another potential cleavage may develop between the industrial and nonindustrial sectors. Those involved in the production of goods are affected by a set of governmental regulations that are less important to those in the service sector. Government policies concerning pollution, raw materials, energy, product safety, and foreign trade have their greatest impact on those involved in manufacturing. Many blue-collar and white-collar workers in the industrial and manufacturing sector may come to agree that increased foreign imports, strict pollution regulations, and strict product safety requirements threaten their economic security. By comparison, those in the service sector rarely will suffer serious and direct economic loss as a result of more stringent government regulation in these areas. This potential industrial–nonindustrial conflict has little or no class basis to it; the relevant socioeconomic divisions are along a horizontal, not vertical, dimension. Conceivably, these cleavages could become a relatively permanent basis of partisan division.

These developments are only possibilities. It seems likely that the economic issues discussed will be important, but it is less certain that relatively permanent cleavages will develop along the occupational lines suggested. For one thing, the existence of common interests and goals is not so immediately obvious to the participants. Unlike the class-based politics of the New Deal era, common political action may not always be a relevant response to these problems. Government em-ployees in one state, for example, may not feel anything in common with those in another state. Similarly, those engaged in automobile manufacturing probably do not feel that their interests coincide with those engaged in the production of pharmaceuticals. What we may have is a myriad of specific economic groups, each with its own inter-ests, with little collective political action among them. This would have a great effect on interest-group politics and the legislative process, but substantial influence on partisan politics would come about only if these economic interests were brought together into a few groupings leading to a restructuring of the party system.

In sum, there is little reason to expect class cleavages to be more pronounced in the future in national politics. The old economic issues, involving questions of social welfare and income redistribution, remain but have a less clear class base. The white working class, having estab-lished itself in economic terms, differs little from the middle class in orientations on some of these issues. New economic issues have become important, and they bear even less relationship to social class. Economic questions are likely to be important in the 1980s, but enduring divisions along socioeconomic lines may be absent.

Another important change in American electoral politics involves the regional shifts that have taken place. The most obvious is the breakup of the solid South. The Democrats remain the majority party in the region, as evidenced by their control of important offices in the region: 90 percent of the state legislators, 75 percent of the congressmen, and 78 percent of the governors are Democrats. But Republican strength in the South, although below the party's levels in the North and West, represents a considerable improvement from earlier levels. Further increases in Republican support may take place. Democratic strength in the South is due in part to the great supply of Democratic office-holders and more established party organization. But these advantages may erode. The Republicans have, in most southern states, attained a critical mass that will allow for growth and development of the party organization. The likely pattern in the 1980s is for the southern Repub-lican vote to grow, although the Democrats will remain the plurality party in the South.

Republican growth in the South may be matched by some decline in the Northeast. Republican strength is moving to the South and West. In part, this involves the growing importance of the so-called Sunbelt in American politics. As a result of population growth and rapid indus-trialization, the Sunbelt states are rivaling the Northeast in importance. The fastest-growing urban areas are located in the South and West.

Politically, the Sunbelt tends to be more conservative, and the Republican Party in this area is considerably to the right of the Northeastern Republicans. The growth of the Republican Party and the growing importance of the Sunbelt correspond to a decline in the moderate-to-liberal Republicanism of the Northeast. The growing power of the southern and western conservative wing of the Republican party was demonstrated by the 1976 Republican presidential nomination conflict. Ford had the support of more established party leaders of the northern states, whereas Reagan's strength was among the activists of the Sunbelt. The fact that Reagan was able to come so close to winning the nomination from the incumbent president suggests how power has shifted in the Republican Party. The future prospect is for even less of a place in the Republican Party for the moderate–liberal elements and for more of a southern and western character to the party.

Since the Sunbelt is the area where Republican strength is still the weakest, regional political shifts during the 1980s may operate to reduce the regional differences that continue to exist in partisan tendencies. Of course, further reduction in partisan differences does not imply that the regions will be politically similar. They may continue to differ in terms of economic interests and political orientations. The South, for example, almost surely will remain more conservative overall in comparison to the Northeast. And the economic interests of the Sunbelt, marked by a surplus of energy sources, a relatively new industrial base, a low rate of unionization, and a substantial amount of agribusiness, surely will be different from those of the Northeast. To some extent, these different economic interests may generate regional conflict, for what operates to the general benefit of one area may be detrimental to other areas. Recent conflict over energy legislation, federal funding formulas, and water control projects have had a strongly regional flavor.

Regional shifts probably will be an important part of any realignment of the party system. Both parties are internally divided, with the southern wings being more conservative and a realignment might reduce these tensions. The more conservative areas of the South and West could provide a solid base of support for a revamped Republican Party, or, as some commentators have suggested, a new conservative party. Similarly, Democratic strength probably would increase in the Northeast and the Great Lakes area. Although regional shifts undoubtedly would be a feature of any realignment, it is unlikely that regional divisions will cause a realignment by themselves. American parties are sufficiently decentralized and flexible to accommodate regional diversity.

Political parties will not realign themselves just because some new arrangement is more logical. Realignment requires a strong catalyst to set off forces that will restructure the party system. The Great Depression did this in the 1930s. At this point it is difficult to foresee what would have a similar effect in the 1980s. It also is difficult to indicate what the features of a new alignment would be. In general, it is easier to specify how the existing system is breaking apart than it is to determine what might replace it.

ELECTORAL POLITICS IN THE 1980s: STALEMATE?

The most likely future scenario is for the present situation to remain. Put simply, political parties will continue in their weakened state and no realignment of the party system will occur. The political issues that appear likely to be important in the near future do not seem capable of breaking the parties apart. Intraparty conflict will occur, perhaps along the economic and regional lines suggested earlier. But there is not the same redundancy of cleavage lines that occurred in the 1930s; groups opposed to fellow Democrats on one issue, for example, may agree with them on another issue. The absence of divisive issues does not imply greater cohesion within the parties, however, for also lacking are the types of issues that bind a party closely together.

The trends in electoral politics that we have outlined should persist into the 1980s. Political parties will remain as the formal organizations through which nominations are made, but whether they will be much more than that remains to be seen. Increasingly, we are likely to find that campaigns are conducted by candidate-oriented organizations supported by ad-hoc coalitions that vary from race to race. Voters will continue to display the high levels of independence, ticket-splitting, and party switching that have characterized their behavior in recent years. Turnout is likely to remain at low levels, perhaps even declining further. The Democrats will remain as the majority party, at least in a nominal sense. In policy terms, partisan conflict in the 1980s probably will best be described as a stalemate, with increasing difficulty in obtaining comprehensive and long-run solutions to the problems facing the country.

We do not wish to end on too pessimistic a note. In some sense, dissatisfaction with political institutions is natural. Indeed, it may even be a healthy sign. Throughout the twentieth century reformers have attempted and often succeeded in altering important features of parties and elections. Our discussion should be taken as an indication that such concerns are as relevant for the 1980s as they have been in earlier periods.

FOR FURTHER READING

Party decomposition and potential realignments are discussed by Walter Dean Burnham, *Critical Elections and the Mainsprings of American Politics.*[17] Different conceptions of the electoral process are considered by Benjamin Page, *Choices and Echoes in Presidential Elections,*[18] and by Austin Ranney, *The Doctrine of Responsible Party Government.*[19]

NOTES

1. Center for Political Studies, *The CPS American National Election Study,* Vol. 1 (Ann Arbor, Michigan: Inter-University Consortium for Political and Social Research, 1977), p. 288.

2. Ibid., pp. 410–411.

3. Everett Carll Ladd, Jr., "The Polls: The Question of Confidence," *Public Opinion Quarterly,* Vol. 40, No. 4 (Winter 1976–1977), pp. 544–552; Arthur H. Miller, "The Majority Party Reunited? A Comparison of the 1972 and 1976 Elections," in Jeff Fishel, ed., *Parties and Elections in an Anti-Party Age,* (Bloomington: Indiana University Press, 1978), p. 131.

4. Thomas E. Cavanagh, "Changes in American Electoral Turnout, 1964–1976" (Paper presented at the 1979 Annual Meeting of the Midwest Political Science Association, Chicago, Illinois, April 19–21, 1979), pp. 14–16.

5. Everett Carll Ladd, Jr., *Where Have All the Voters Gone?* (New York: Norton, 1978), p. 62.

6. Michael J. Malbin, "Election Day Registration: Can it Really Make a Difference?" *National Journal,* May 7, 1977, p. 31. It should be noted that Minnesota had a relatively high turnout rate even before the adoption of the new registration procedures.

7. Ibid., pp. 32–33.

8. The term seems to have been coined by Walter Dean Burnham. See his *Critical Elections and the Mainsprings of American Poltics* (New York: Norton, 1970).

9. Ladd, *Where Have All the Voters Gone?,* p. xviii.

10. Benjamin I. Page, *Choices and Echoes in Presidential Elections* (Chicago: University of Chicago Press, 1978), p. 194.

11. Ibid., 222.

12. Walter Dean Burnham, "American Politics in the 1970s: Beyond Party?" in Louis Maisel and Paul M. Sacks, eds., *The Future of Political Parties,* (Beverly Hills, California: Sage, 1975), p. 263.

13. Michael J. Malbin, "Labor, Business and Money: A Post-Election Analysis," *National Journal*, March 19, 1977, p. 38.

14. Burnham, *Critical Elections*, p. 133.

15. Burnham, "American Politics in the 1970s," pp. 248–256.

16. Charles L. Prysby, "Mass Policy Orientation on Economic Issues in Post-Industrial America," *Journal of Politics*, Vol. 41, No. 2 (May, 1979), pp. 543–565.

17. New York: Norton, 1970.

18. Chicago: University of Chicago Press, 1978.

19. Urbana: University of Illinois Press, 1962.

Index